Understanding Teenage Girls

Understanding Teenage Girls

Culture, Identity, and Schooling

Horace R. Hall

with Andrea Brown-Thirston

ROWMAN & LITTLEFIELD EDUCATION
A division of
ROWMAN & LITTLEFIELD PUBLISHERS, INC.
Lanham • New York • Toronto • Plymouth, UK

Published by Rowman & Littlefield Education
A division of Rowman & Littlefield Publishers, Inc.
A wholly owned subsidary of The Rowman & Littlefield Publishing Group, Inc.
4501 Forbes Boulevard, Suite 200, Lanham, Maryland 20706
http://www.rowmaneducation.com

Estover Road, Plymouth PL6 7PY, United Kingdom

British Library Cataloguing in Publication Information Available

Library of Congress Cataloging-in-Publication Data

Hall, Horace R.
  Understanding teenage girls : culture, identity, and schooling / Horace R. Hall with Andrea Brown-Thirston.
      p. cm.
  Includes bibliographical references.
  ISBN 978-1-61048-050-5 (cloth : alk. paper) -- ISBN 978-1-61048-051-2 (pbk. : alk. paper) -- ISBN 978-1-61048-052-9 (electronic)
  1. Teenage girls--United States--Social conditions. 2. Teenage girls--Education--United States. I. Brown-Thirston, Andrea, 1973- II. Title.
  HQ798.H324 2011
  305.235'2086940977311--dc22
                                        2010037150

For

Sophia

Contents

Acknowledgments

The authors would first like to acknowledge and praise the most High for making this book, as well as *all* things, possible. We were guided by faith and grace in completing it.

A very special "thank you" to all of the young women who co-authored this book by sharing their thoughts, experiences, laughter, and even tears. You forever have our respect and admiration for your involvement.

Our sincerest appreciation to those who gave their support and guidance in making this work a reality—Elaine Agusto; Steven Callen (MP); Todd Campbell; Benjamin Churchill; Lynette Danley (Sankofa); Ana Elise Delgado (*amor y revolución*); Sara Echevarria; Elizabeth Fyffe; Joseph Gardner; Joyce Gilmore; Ayani Good; Samantha Hall (chin-chin); Samuel Kingston Hall; Cyle, Chaundra, and Dave Harrison; Jean Miller; Nicole Ruiz; Bernadette Sanchez; Eleshia Smith; Beverly Trezek; and Sonia Wright.

We would also like to acknowledge DePaul University's School of Education for helping to fund the research that went into this book. The views expressed in this text are the authors' and are not necessarily shared by DePaul University or its School of Education.

To our publisher, Rowman & Littlefield Education, most notably Vice President and Editorial Director Tom Koerner—your unwavering patience and constant encouragement truly helped to bring our work to this point.

Finally, to all of our comrades—the work before us pales in comparison to the solidarity between us. Fight the good fight and we will get there. *C'est la guerre et nous sommes dans la guerre.*

Foreword

Many people believe that racism and sexism no longer exist in the United States. Respectfully, one could argue that point as women, particularly women of color, have made significant strides in the realms of business, government, and education. More specifically, Latina and African American females presently serve at the highest levels of the military; are major stakeholders in professional football and basketball teams; hold appointments as chancellors, provosts, and presidents of colleges and universities; and are chief executive officers and senior vice presidents of Fortune 500 companies.

Of course, how can we forget Michelle Obama, the first African American woman to serve as first lady of the United States, or Sonia Sotomayor, the first Latina judge appointed to the U.S. Supreme Court? These women, in their own right, earned their current status, appointments, and/or leadership roles based on their intellect, commitment to education, and tireless efforts to heal and revitalize their respective communities.

Honoring and celebrating the accomplishments of minority women and the positions they hold have been and continue to be interrupted due to the intersection of their identities as engendered persons of color. Society at large wrestles with the fact or outright refusal to acknowledge that, as Adrien Katherine Wing asserts in *Critical Race Feminism*, "women of color are simply not white women plus some ineffable and secondary characteristic, such as skin tone added on." And, despite existing laws and policies such as affirmative action, equal rights amendments, and Title IX (which are all under attack), the reality is that changing laws does not immediately equate with changing mindsets.

Whether it was the vilifying cartoon image of First Lady Obama on the cover of the July 21, 2008, New Yorker edition, sporting an afro, carrying a machine gun, and giving President Obama "some dap," or the congressional hearing, also known around the nation as the "hostile, interrogation and cross-examination," of Sotomayor before she was sworn in as judge on August 8, 2009, some people may argue that these isolated events do not constitute inquiry into the lives of Latina and African-American girls and young women.

However, to the contrary, many females of color encounter daily misogynistic media messages, achievement gaps, abusive relationships, attempted suicide, homelessness, teen pregnancy, overcrowding in special education classrooms (often misdiagnosed as speech or behavior disorders because English is not their first language), truancy, gang violence, human trafficking, and juvenile detention centers, which often feed the school-to-prison pipelines and alternative schools placements that we see today.

If, at the highest levels of society, Black and Hispanic adult women are being vilified, marginalized, and silenced, then why can't we understand that it happens at younger ages as well? Hall and Brown-Thirston critically unpack this very question by highlighting voices usually lost in traditional scholarship. *Understanding Teenage Girls: Culture, Identity and Schooling* offers a collection of testimonials that, given the murky data on black and brown girls, makes this work a rare truth-telling text, embracing and illuminating gray areas in research.

In comparison to every other adolescent female population (Asian-American, Native American, Pacific Islander, third- and fourth-generation Middle Easterners, and yes, White females), African-American and Latina girls endure, at higher rates, the impact of faulty educational policies, ahistorical curriculum, and figurative framings that diminish or disregard their experiences. The state of these crises are all supported by national rates and statistics that reveal not only that race *still* matters but that gender intersected with black and brown skin is prevalent even now.

The exploration of how society has historically characterized femininity and the effects of that influence regarding how African-American, Chicana, and Puerto Rican girls see themselves continues to go underresearched and dismissed as critical inquiry. The need to examine the stories behind the statistics, the narratives behind the numbers, and the hypocrisy disguised is where we unquestionably instigate points of contention.

Hall and Brown-Thirston's work explicitly negates ideologies such as "assimilation is necessary," "girls of color are apathetic," "one group's pain is greater than the other," and "blaming the victim," which all encompass a deficit foundation. *Understanding Teenage Girls* serves as revolutionary work illustrating how deeply embedded expectations of "White femininity" are unfair and often serve as forms of oppression that affect and confound adolescent girls of color to their detriment.

Black and brown girls across the country ask, "Why are we not viewed as precious, set apart, deserving of love and entitled to the same level of respect given to White girls?" Even how black and brown girls are engaged at home, at school, in their communities, and society at large, because of the connection of their skin color and gender, needs to be discussed with more breadth and depth.

Can you imagine being told that you are *not* the representation of "deity, worthy of the best, pure, good, and a pedestal that should be placed above all others"? And further not have those ideas reinforced by those closest to you, including family and educators? This is just one of the countless reasons as to why girls and women of color need spaces to redefine femininity in ways that speak to their racial and cultural experiences.

Broadening our scope of scholarship, *Understanding Teenage Girls* strategically suspends ego and traditional traits associated with the role of researchers and participants. In doing so, the young women here are within a space to coconstruct knowledge, be experts on issues that plague their communities, and reclaim the power of their identities and voices by sharing their narratives.

How the African-American and Latina girls in this book view, live, and survive in their homes, schools, and society is identifiable in any language. Though rarely acknowledged as rigorous research, the qualitative inquiry in this text is liberating. The girls spoke "their truths," because they were confident that they were being heard. This unique approach has interdisciplinary appeal and applicability representing the future of teaching and learning.

Even after twenty years of working in the field of education, I still ask myself, what am I doing in the Academy? I am an African-American female who grew up on the west side of Chicago. Throughout my educational journey, I can only recall a handful of moments where I felt safe and free enough to say what was really on my mind. I still struggle with the "Imposter Syndrome," yet books like *Understanding Teenage Girls* reassure me that my presence and perspective matter.

From this reading, I better understand how as a scholar of color, I can interrogate with integrity and provide tangible examples of how to investigate the core and source of issues without objectifying the people affected by them. Hall and Brown-Thirston's philosophy of "no hierarchy, but solidarity" supports authentic reciprocity of researchers and participants. It is an interdisciplinary roadmap for educators, administrators, and community organizations that examine historic and contemporary societal perspectives, frameworks, and practices affecting African-American and Latina adolescent females.

As a scholar-activist, the questions I often wrestle with are "What out-of-classroom factors influence black and brown girls in-class levels of academic performance?" and "What factors aid or impede the mobility of black and brown girls throughout the pre-K–12 school pipeline?" We know there is a plethora of inter- and intradynamics at the macrolevel (e.g., federal funding, immigration policies, teacher shortages), but the problems at the microlevels (e.g., the culture of households and family values) are just as important to consider.

One of my students made a comment that I found compelling and relentlessly profound: "Why do I have to censor what I say in classroom spaces, when what happens to me in life is not censored?" Not surprised by any of my students' intellect, the statement took on a new meaning. What would research look like if people had real opportunities to express their thoughts and feelings unapologetically?

Are we brave enough, humble enough, vulnerable enough, as faculty, educators, administrators, families, community organizers, to listen to unadulterated moments? What type of environment does one have to make for people to disclose their innermost thoughts without fear of being judged, misrepresented, or misunderstood?

Hall and Brown-Thirston protect the young women in this research from having to care about offending others or from the need to alter what they believe is necessary to say without being perceived as a "threat." This book models humanistic, constructivist, and unconventional inquiry without compromising academic integrity or rigor. There is something to be said about scholarship that has the insight and ability to set aside ego, sit down, shut up, and let the participants tell their stories.

Lynette L. Danley, PhD

Preface

Even in the twenty-first century, age-old societal notions of femininity still prevail. Deeply seated images and representations of women inform girls, at very early ages and in nearly every society, that to be feminine means being, in part, quiet, passive, delicate, and dependent.

The adoption of these predetermined qualities occurs mostly on an unconscious level as they are systemic of social and cultural traditions pervasive within communities and the broader society. Although a prevailing archetype of femininity exists, some African-American, Chicana, and Puerto Rican females display a set of related, as well as disparate, behaviors that imply intracultural and individual variances within the nature of this phenomenon.

In order to fully grasp the social construction of femininity, we must first recognize that it is historically and conceptually rooted in a White middle-class perspective—a position largely preoccupied with gender and that overlooks privileges associated with Whiteness.

As this framework fails to acknowledge economic discrimination experienced by women of color,[1] both past and present, discussions on femininity must also incorporate a focus on class, adding another layer of consciousness to the multidimensionality of adolescent female identity development—the moment when these young girls come to realize how societal barriers, linked to race, class, and gender, have a profound impact on their life chances and personal goals.

For most of the twentieth century, White middle-class mothers occupied the role of stay-at-home caregiver, while husbands functioned as the principal wage earner. Within these homes, daughters typically worked alongside their mothers, participating in domestic duties that instilled conventional feminine expectations and conduct.

Black daughters, from working-class, single-parent households, witnessed their mothers working outside the home, often for long hours and for modest pay. Based upon their family unit structure and class status, these girls, within their own cultural community, developed a contrasting ideological set of womanhood—one that was (and still is) confounded by racial and class variations.

Though there is a lesser amount of literature on gender construction among Hispanics, for Chicanas and Latinas in America some scholars contend that gender roles are informed by the cultural value of *familismo*. This tradition can be described as a sense of obligation and identification to the nuclear and extended family, with the needs of the collective, at times, superseding individual desires.

Some Chicanas and Latinas are absorbed into this deterministic framework that characterizes males as independent, strong, and dominant (*machismo*) and females as reliant, obedient, and pure (*marianismo*). Scholars have noted that the adoption and maintenance of these cultural gender scripts can be disrupted when individuals are faced with assimilation in American society (e.g., class elevation, taking on a new language, social interaction, and/or academic attainment).

Despite conventional models of femininity, tension exists in the behaviors that African-American and Hispanic adolescent females demonstrate. While some closely adhere to traditional gender prescriptions, others visibly step outside the lines of the gender box. These performed "deviations" have been acknowledged as conscious and unconscious opposition against a perceived sexist, racist, and classist society.

As adolescence marks a period in human development where abstract thinking comes to the forefront, we must recognize that females of color are able to perceptively discern, as well as accept or reject, social mores and ideologies that affect their overall identity development. For those young women opting to challenge the notion of "sugar and spice and everything nice" or defy expectations of *machismo*, they do so for the sake of—and even at the risk of—protecting their own distinct voice and sense of femaleness.

In educational settings, recent conversations revolving around minority children tend to focus on the plight of African-American and Latino boys. These youth, mostly researched in urban centers, are overrepresented in special education classrooms and are referred for disciplinary measures with far greater frequency than their White and Asian counterparts. Black and Hispanic males are not only perceived as being the most resistant to formal education but, within the larger society, are also stigmatized as being rebellious, deviant, and unreachable.

While it is vital for communities to understand and act upon extreme issues surrounding males of color, our fixation on them often relegates the realities of African-American, Chicana, and Puerto Rican females to the margins. As we endeavor to comprehend the multitude of obstacles encountered by boys, we must also become more responsive to the challenges faced by girls and how both gender experiences are inextricably linked.

So what are the life experiences for some African-American and Hispanic teenage girls with respect to school and home life? Within the classroom setting, it has been noted that girls, in general, are less of a behavioral problem than boys, thus having a better relationship with teachers. This perspective is grounded in the age-old social construction of gender that frames boys as boisterous and aggressive and girls as silent and passive.

The engrained perception of femaleness, as "ladylike" or "womanly," is highly contested, however, in the presence of some females of color, who may not completely subscribe to this middle-class, Eurocentric standard. Consequently, their behaviors, within school settings, are viewed as inappropriate as educators frequently label them as loud, feisty, unintelligent, delinquent, or hostile. Discipline measures are often used to force these girls back into the rigid gender box of White femininity, only compelling them to further resist academic spaces.

Beyond the school setting, we find similar labels that tend to emphasize the "deficits" and "pathologies" of females of color. The dominant imagery presented portrays them as hypersexual, disruptive, antisocial, psychologically unstable, substance abusing, or government dependent. Even though some endure the barriers associated with low socioeconomic status or single parenthood, the persistent assessment is that the life of the average urban young woman of color is wrought by poverty, promiscuity, motherhood, and social maladjustment.

These devaluing impressions potentially impact how educators teach these students and how school counselors and social workers care and connect with them. As long as the infinite ethnic identities of African-American and Hispanic females continue to be measured against stringent monocultural yardsticks that narrowly define who they are, educators and youth workers will be left with very little to engage and empower these young people and to see them other than the "at-risk" labels that codify their lives.

Understanding Teenage Girls: Culture, Identity, and Schooling focuses on an assortment of social phenomena that negatively and positively impact young females of color—adolescent development, gender socialization, teenage pregnancy, media stereotyping, body image, community violence, family support systems, schooling, and mentoring.

The authors elected to represent African-American, Mexican-American, and Puerto Rican female students together, in a single volume, to not necessarily stress cultural differences, but instead to highlight their commonalities and shared perspectives on the phenomena listed above. Despite the age range of our participants (16–19), we also chose to refer to them as young or adolescent women due to the fact that they themselves see their level of maturity and life experiences at the midpoint between girlhood and woman-hood.

All fourteen participants featured in this book are residents of Chicago, Illinois. Eleven attend an alternative high school that enrolls students labeled as "at-risk" for academic failure for such reasons as poor school attendance, low reading test scores, delinquency, behavioral problems, teenage pregnancy, and financial burdens related to socioeconomic status. These students had previously been enrolled in traditional public schools, but had either dropped out or had been expelled.

The remaining three participants attend a charter school that serves mainly low-income, African-American families. The lived realities of these students are in no way meant to generalize a population. Although their experiences might resonate with other girls and young women, we consider their voices to be unique and indispensable in guiding our thoughts and analyses around some of the critical issues that confront Black and Hispanic female students on a daily basis.

Understanding Teenage Girls: Culture, Identity, and Schooling presents the multiple life worlds that these young women inhabit for the purpose of seeing them beyond fixed and limited social stigmas. Our primary goal for this volume is to underscore those cultural and contextual factors that weigh heavily upon their everyday experiences, while also understanding the intricacy of the adolescent phase that they are in.

Even though issues associated with self-image, gender/sexual scripts, maternity, peer relationships, as well as relational aggression and victimization, can be surveyed across "femaleness," this book inserts these phenomena within the framework of what it means growing up female, Black or Hispanic, urban, and working class.

In many instances, the daily obstacles that our participants encounter are nonaccessible to other females of different class status, such as Miley Cyrus, Paris Hilton, Kim Kardashian, or Lindsay Lohan. Indeed, the conflation of race and class creates an additional set of barriers that are powerfully manifested through insufficient forms of social capital and economic resources.

In accessing what it means for our participants to be young women of color, this book's second objective is to unearth their often hidden or un-shared epistemologies. Undeniably, every student brings a variety of issues into schools and classrooms. The young women presented in this volume openly discuss their personal concerns, providing multiple clues to their location within the intersection of race, class, and gender.

Weaved throughout chapters are their voices, speaking to a collection of beliefs, judgments, and attitudes that shape their respective identities. By positioning these students at the heart of sociological inquiry, we seek to not only produce a more comprehensive picture of how they construct meaning in their world, but also redress societal misinterpretations that label them as inferior.

Joined with their narratives are the authors' own analyses guided by our extensive teaching and mentoring experiences, as well as contemporary research from the fields of education, counseling, psychology, nursing, and anthropology. We also submit a range of practical methods and resources that can be used for assisting African-American and Latina girls in building healthy attitudes and a personal sense of agency.

In addition to expanding the knowledge of how young females of color become devalued by society, we attempt to explain how they handle adversity, persevere, and, quite simply, live out their lives. The young women featured here have incredible odds stacked against them. But they, just as anyone else, desire to actualize their hopes and dreams. Hence, the third aim of this text is to unpack the culturally ambiguous nature of resiliency.

The authors are well aware of conventional norm-referenced models that misconstrue and aggregate people of color into "deficit" and "at-risk" social groupings based upon cultural differences. Such interpretations not only subtract human dimension away from minority groups, but also fail to illuminate the distinctive capacities that diverse cultures possess in translating their own problems and constructively acting upon them.

While presently there is no book on the market that presumes our exact focus, the basis of this volume flows within the same scholarship as Bianca Guzmán (*Latina Girls: Voices of Adolescent Strength in the U.S.*, 2006); Venus E. Evans-Winters (*Teaching Black Girls: Resiliency in Urban Classrooms*, 2005); and Dierdre Glenn Paul (*Talkin' Back: Raising and Educating Resilient Black Girls*, 2003)—works that have been instrumental in critically investigating the societal barriers experienced by pre- and adolescent girls, while offering realistic approaches for assisting them.

As there is a profusion of research that explores why females of color fail or succeed academically, there is less examination of those dynamics that foster their resiliency. *Understanding Teenage Girls* responds to this paucity by presenting the lives of African-American, Chicana, and Puerto Rican females with less pathology and more promise, identifying those challenges confronting young women of color, but also noting how, through various supportive measures they can (and do) overcome day-to-day obstacles.

Although there has been a proliferation of voice research and reporting, the articulations of working-class, adolescent females of color have been largely absent from this emerging literature. With regard to what presently exists, this volume parallels the work of Rosie Molinary (*Hijas Americanas: Beauty, Body Image, and Growing Up Latina*, 2007) and Iris Jacob (*My Sisters' Voices: Teenage Girls of Color Speak Out*, 2002). These authors tender a collection of narratives and essays that call attention to the often "invisible" lives of Black and Hispanic girls.

Through primarily student interviews, *Understanding Teenage Girls* brings readers closer to the concerns of females of color by sharing their personal stories around culture and society, hope and desire, conflict and change. These students' lives hold the potential for engaging readers, perhaps for the first time, in coming to know the range of social identities that make up urban, adolescent girls of color. This book serves as informational text, intertwining research and analysis with student reality as a means of compelling readers to rethink their assumptions and revise their perceptions around this marginalized social group.

Understanding Teenage Girls is meant for *all* readers. It is, however, especially intended for teachers and students of education, psychology, sociology, and social work. Teacher educators will find this volume useful for undergraduate and graduate courses related to educational psychology, curriculum and instruction, the sociology of education, human development and growth, and middle-level and secondary education. The subject matter presented in this text will prove beneficial for students employing disciplinary lenses of gender and ethnic studies, multiculturalism, feminism, and critical urban pedagogy.

This work has also been designed to assist youth advocates and parents desiring to familiarize themselves with the needs, issues, and concerns of young women of color. Finally, the book is for and about adolescent girls. With that in mind, we hope that in these pages girls can read of parallel struggles, yet find direction and resolve as they walk *their* own personal road to womanhood.

Chapter 1 opens with a discussion of gender norms and adolescent development from psychological and biological perspectives. Our participants offer their perspectives on what it means to be a girl versus being a woman. The authors provide further information and analyses around supplementary themes such as: post-secondary educational attainment; teenage drop out and pregnancy; financial independence; and the foster care system.

Chapter 2 looks at stereotypes of women of color and our participant viewpoints on media representations. The authors focus on body image and eating disorders, as well as where our young participants find their support base and personal power in the face of gender, racial, and class stereotyping.

Chapter 3 explores girls mirroring traditional masculine behaviors and why girls and young women are engaged in classicallyl viewed male anti-social activities (e.g., gang membership and fighting). The authors also examine racial tensions between African-American and Hispanic teens in Chicago public schools and neighborhoods, as well as relational aggression and victimization.

Chapter 4 studies the importance of education and schooling from the perspectives of our participants. The authors discuss parental involvement in education and the role of familial and nonfamilial support bases—mothers, fathers, grandparents, and community members—in building resiliency in young people.

Chapter 5 observes those in-school dynamics that negatively impact the lives of the young women represented in this book—racial micro-aggressions, harsh discipline codes of conduct, biased teacher expectations, and culturally myopic school curriculum.

Chapter 6 presents a discussion of school-based mentoring for adolescent females of color. The authors submit a distinct mentoring model undergirded by three programmatic strands. Student reactions to being involved in mentoring programs and their importance are also undertaken.

Chapter 7 concludes larger discussions from previous chapters and submits thoughts from the authors and "words of wisdom," expressed by the participants, to other girls and young women.

NOTE

1. Throughout this book, women or females of color will exclusively refer to girls and young women of African-American, Mexican-American, and Puerto Rican backgrounds. "People of color," in general, is an inclusive category consisting of African, Asian, Latin, Native American, and those ethnic groups residing in underdeveloped countries. Black and African-American will be used interchangeably. Chicana/o refers to Mexican-Americans or persons of Mexican heritage and will be used in this book to specifically denote this group. The terms *Hispanic* and *Latina/o*, as more generic references, will be used intermittently to describe both Mexican-American and Puerto Rican groups.

Chapter One

Girls Will Be Women

One is not born a woman, one becomes one. —*Simone de Beauvoir*

The true worth of a race must be measured by the character of its womanhood. —*Mary McLeod Bethune*

Adolescence is marked as a period in human development between the ages fourteen and eighteen. During these years, young people from *all* backgrounds are experiencing vigorous transitions—from physical to psychological and from social to emotional. Despite the fact that puberty typically begins before fourteen (in boys and girls), it tends to be the most associated phenomenon with this age group. While puberty imparts both sexes with a set of comparable physical changes (e.g., growth spurt, harder bones, oilier skin, higher testosterone and estrogen levels, and arm, leg, and pubic hair growth), it also poses a mixture of contrasting ones.

For instance, males generally develop chest hair and broader shoulders, produce sperm, and have a greater proportion of body muscle to fat. Females, on the other hand, have an increased proportion of body fat to muscle, develop breasts and broader hips, and experience monthly menstruation. Although the onset of puberty usually occurs earlier with girls (age eight) than with boys (age nine and a half), the duration to complete these physical changes, for either sex, varies between two to five years or even longer.

From a psychological perspective, adolescence is considered to be the dawning of a conscious and unconscious search for the self. Identity research generated over the past forty years[1] from psychologists such as Erik Erikson, Anna Freud, and James Marcia, points to adolescence as a time when youth begin intensely questioning who they are, while developing an emergent sense of autonomy. This push for independence ought not to be viewed as a total disconnection from guardians, but rather an increased connection to the

1

peer group. In other words, most adolescents remain relatively close to their families, but also seek to become intimate with significant others outside the home.

With cognitive capacities growing, abstract thinking comes to the forefront and adolescents find themselves deliberating over their interests and personalities, as well as their social role and how others see them. This search for "the true me" becomes further complicated by a burgeoning sexual identity (via puberty). This pushes teenagers to compare different aspects of themselves with that of same- and opposite-sex peer groups as they form relationships based on friendship, trust, romance, and intimacy.

Preoccupied with constant evaluation and reflection, the adolescent identity is in continuous flux, engendering feelings of anxiety, confusion, uncertainty, and even isolation. Even within the most confident of teens, we can still see a level of insecurity and angst. Nevertheless, it is through peer and adult interactions that young folks are able to enhance their social and emotional capacities, expand their autonomy, and further mold their behaviors and personalities, all while discovering who they are in the adult world, if only for that moment.

Despite the general framework surrounding adolescent physical growth and identity formation, there still exist distinct cultural factors that influence how various adolescent males and females develop socially. Prior to reaching their teens, it is believed that young people have already been engaged in everyday cultural practices that function to shape their gender identities.

For instance, within some traditional Euro-American families, girls typically work closely with their mothers on tasks that comprise household affairs, as well as tending to the needs of others (e.g., parents, siblings, or extended family members). Boys, on the other hand, are taught to be more self-reliant and sufficient, whether they are working alongside their mother or father.

By the time the sexes enter adolescence, gender socialization is considered complete. Boys come to understand the necessity of gaining independence from the family, in order to explore and master the world and to later become the provider of their own household. Girls, having formed nurturing, interdependent relationships with their parents during childhood, tend to take less drastic measures in achieving autonomy as they intuitively recognize the import of remaining in "the nest" and maintaining close bonds with family members.

With respect to gender socialization, parallels can be drawn between White, Hispanic, and Black cultures. For example, among Chicanos and Latinos, there exists the tradition of *machismo*, where males are taught to stress dominance over females and to protect and provide for the family. Alternatively, the cultural value of *marianismo* places females into roles of child care, home management, and emotional support for boyfriends and husbands.

Similar to White and Hispanic males, African-American boys are also informed that being a "real man" means being self-reliant and in control. Although Black males receive the similar message of "masculine as dominant," some are not communicated the entire script of masculine as also "provider."[2] This partial instruction can directly affect how Black girls view manhood, while simultaneously constructing their own role as a woman. Cultural scholars assert that given the history of social and economic challenges faced by African-Americans, Black women have not only had to develop a sense of assertiveness and self-reliance, in their own right, but also have had to take on the dual role of home provider and caregiver.

Regardless of one's cultural lens, the adolescent world is far more expansive for boys than for girls. On the road to manhood, boys receive certain privileges that reinforce the expectation that they should be in control over people and situations in their lives. Girls are engulfed by slighter expectations—ones that do not necessarily call for them to be dominant, to master the world, to become an explorer, an executive, or a political leader.

This is not to say that girls have neither the need nor the desire to undertake such roles—indeed they do. Rather, it is to stress how norms and expectations, across cultures, send girls ingraining, restrictive messages as to who they are and what their duty as a woman should be. When girls learn that their professional goals are regarded as socially unacceptable for their gender, they intuitively sense that a power dynamic is at work and that males are in command of it.

Some girls even become aware of how gender arrangements function to undervalue their mind, body, and self-worth. Depending on their culture, girls and young women may respond to gender norms in any number of ways—some challenge them by redefining womanhood as they see fit, disregarding what is socially unacceptable; others remain persistent in pursuing their girlhood dreams, while still embracing conventional feminine codes; and then there are those who fully adhere to traditional femininity, which, in some cases, means relinquishing their dreams, their goals, and even their self-esteem.

The authors of this book sat down and spoke with fourteen female high school students from Chicago, Illinois. We informed them of our purpose for writing this book, and they were open and honest and let us in. We met with them in groups of three to four and encouraged them to freely express their ideas and discuss whatever they felt was important. Their interviews were audio-recorded, transcribed, and then later analyzed.

One could mistakenly blanket these students as simply adolescent mothers, wards of the state, school dropouts, juvenile offenders, or ex-gangbangers. On the contrary, their words and experiences help to dispel inaccurate social labels as they are clearly resilient, intellectual, courageous, reflective, humorous, caring, and frail young women still determining who they are and what their social role might be.

As researchers, despite being African-American ourselves, we are well sure that we could have initially been viewed, by the participants, as privileged, middle-class academicians entering into a different life world. Aside from this possible characterization, we desired to do more than just social inquiry. Our efforts here are a genuine attempt to see life through these young women's eyes for the purpose of not only understanding their individual complexities, but also to better inform policies, programs, and curriculum designed to identify and address many of the critical issues surrounding females of color.

The next section begins with the first question posed to several of our participants: *What is the difference between being a girl versus being a woman?*

GIRL VS. WOMAN

Halle

Halle is seventeen and African-American. She sees herself as "outgoing, respectful, goofy, open, mature, honest, and motivated." With her smudged glasses and baby face, it is hard to believe that she is expecting her first child in six months. Halle's future goal is to graduate at the end of the school year and attend college, all while "responsibly raising" her baby. She takes pleasure in learning new things, watching movies, and being with her family and baby's father.

> A woman is strong, independent, well-respected by peers, respects herself, and just carrying herself the right way, and then basically doing what's right.

Lapita

Lapita is eighteen and Puerto Rican. She describes herself as "hopeful, spontaneous, and sexy." Her goals for the future are to graduate from high school, earn a college scholarship, and become a law enforcement officer. She loves to play sports, even though she admits to being "lazy." She says that she enjoys having a good time and being "smart and responsible," but needs to work on her short temper. In her group interview, Lapita dominated conversation. There is definitely a spark and liveliness about her.

> A woman is when you own your own stuff. You got your job, you got your own house, your characteristics, how you carry yourself. Like a young woman, or a lady,

wouldn't use profanity to anybody or expose herself to the public in a certain type of way. So I think it's all about the way you carry yourself.

Mya

Mya is eighteen years of age and African-American. She describes herself as "smart, happy, and a Pisces." Her goal is to graduate from high school and continue raising her daughter. Mya states that she wants to find a good job and a nice apartment. She likes to play with her daughter and go to different places around town with friends and family. Mya has a very strong personality—self-confident and wise. She is surely a Rosa Parks or Shirley Chisholm in-the-making.

> The difference between a girl and a woman is that a girl is just a little bit younger. A woman is like when you got a job, you're in your own place. You're doing everything for yourself and then a girl is like kind of the same thing but you just a little bit lower. You still in your parent's house, you got to respect that, or whatever, and that's just being a girl. But a woman is like if a guy approaches me and he slap me on my butt, I'll turn around and really say something, but I won't use profanity. I would be like, "Excuse me, sir, you ain't supposed to put your hands on me like that." That's feminine, instead of going about like, "Yeah, you ain't supposed to put your dag-gone hands on me." It's all in the way they set their self out there.

The responses above illuminate a dividing line between girlhood and womanhood that our participants qualify with a set of comparable traits and behaviors. Their ideas on womanhood, we believe, are not informed by a singular dynamic (e.g., race, class, or gender), but rather exist as a confluence of social and cultural definitions around what it means to be a woman.

With regard to their opinions on womanhood, Mya states, "It's all in the way they set their self out there." Lapita affirms by adding, "Like a young woman, or a lady, wouldn't use profanity to anybody or expose herself to the public in a certain type of way." These observations encapsulate the larger societal belief that being a woman requires having respect for one's self and for others.

More specifically, they indicate how a woman should carry herself publicly, in appearance and in speech. In addition to their sentiments on self-respect, all three students point to "independence" as another integral characteristic. Lapita and Mya consider independence as being employed and having your own place to live.

While their responses are indeed definitions of womanhood, their comments also speak to their conceptualizations of becoming an adult. That is, they see financial freedom and independent living as markers of adulthood. This outlook, of course, is not exclusive to young women of color, but in fact reflects the ideals of other adolescents from various cultural communities.

What must be observed here is that the students' impression of woman-hood and self-reliance is also linked to their academic goals (as seen in their profiles). All three are striving to finish high school, with Halle and Lapita intending to enter into college. These objectives, certainly, suggest not only a desire to heighten their independence, but also to elevate their social mobility as education is often deemed as a vehicle for advancement. This outlook becomes a critical point of discussion.

Even as the alternative school that these students attend touts successful transitions into college, data on Chicago alternative school graduation rates confirm that less than 25 percent of students graduate, much less attend and pay for postsecondary education. The disheartening reality is that for return-ing students, like the ones above, alternative schools tend to be their last chance for a high school diploma. If they do not satisfy graduation require-ments by the age of twenty-one, they involuntarily age-out of the alternative school setting, as they are no longer entitled to a free public education.

With the above in mind, we need to be aware of those obstacles that make the procurement of a diploma challenging for alternative school students. For example, the majority who enroll are years behind academically; some suffer from low-school esteem; their school utilizes outdated books and other re-sources; they are taught by faculty who are untrained in meeting their specif-ic needs; or, as in the case of Halle and Mya, they are adolescent parents,[3] which, undeniably, creates a series of additional stresses and distractions.

Students of color, from traditional schools in primarily impoverished ar-eas, grapple with similar issues. Educational researchers have contended that such factors not only make it more difficult for these students to fulfill state academic standards, as well as graduation requirements, but also force them out of the traditional school environment in the first place.

Across the United States, approximately half of African-American stu-dents and 60 percent of Latino students graduate on time with a high school diploma. In the Chicago Public School (CPS) system, African-American and Hispanic secondary students have the lowest graduation rates as compared to the national average for these groups.

In 2009, CPS had a 49 percent student dropout rate—a majority of whom were low-income African-American and Hispanic males. This has drawn grave concern among educators and parents alike given that CPS's student body is approximately 45 percent Black, 41 percent Hispanic, 9 percent White, 3 percent Asian, and less than 1 percent Native American. CPS also has the second-largest low-income student population of the eleven sur-rounding Chicagoland districts.

With regard to pursuing formal education beyond high school, the U.S. Department of Education reported a 21 percent increase (between 1990 and 2002) in tenth grade students' desire to attend college. However, more recent studies have shown that many Black and Hispanic students are underprepared for college-level courses. Most of these youth end up taking remedial classes (completing graduation requirements by the age of twenty-four), while some disconnect from university life altogether.[4]

In *Smart and Sassy: The Inner Strengths of Inner-City Black Girls*,[5] Joyce West Stevens writes:

> Given present-day social mores, the expectation that a college education is needed to compete successfully in today's economy places poor youth at great disadvantage when entering adulthood since most are not likely to attend college. Additionally, most poor youth are not likely to receive even postsecondary training to become mid-level skilled entrants into the labor economy. Even when African-Americans attend college, they are the least likely to attend elitist schools or to benefit from the social status networks indigenous to privileged colleges and universities. . . . One wonders if American society has narrowly defined socially sanctioned opportunity pathways to achieve adulthood status. Restricted trajectories for adulthood preparation say much about society's commitment to youth. (149)

West Stevens insightfully captures the impasse that we, as a society, force low-income students of color into. When we present them with educational requirements, but fail to provide them with educational building blocks to be viable in the global economy, we constrict their financial in-roads, as well as their anticipated adulthood independence. We dangle the proverbial carrot right in front of them, and then remove it before they ever have time to grasp it.

In 2009, there were 1.2 million dropouts nationwide. Of this figure, only 37 percent were employed. Most of the young people who do not graduate from high schools are short of fundamental job skills, as well as adequate literacy and math capabilities to gain sound employment. While some are out of work, others are not even looking.

No doubt young people from disjointed communities become viscerally aware of the societal message they are being sent: *They do not matter and others are worth more.* Facing inequities, adolescent females of color, like the ones above, espouse a level of hope and resilience that prevents them from devaluing their self and their abilities. The authors became quite aware of this during our time with them and saw it as a foremost trait in virtually every student that we interviewed.

Maria

Maria is first generation Mexican-American and a returning student at nineteen. She sees herself as "respectful, responsible, and independent." She intends to graduate at the end of the academic year and "not just go to college, but finish it." Maria says that she loves math, reading, and taking care of her baby. In her group interview, Maria was quiet and modest with mature countenance.

It means a lot to be a woman because not a lot of guys have figured out that we are so much. They just think, "Well, you gotta cook, you gotta do this, you gotta do that, while I'm not going to do nothing." And it's not like that because we suffer much more than guys. I mean, you try having a baby. Try raising it by yourself. Try supporting it. Even though you have the man's support, sometimes, if the man gets mad, he won't give you any money or he'll just walk away, whether you have babies or not. But, in the meantime, you're not stuck with your babies. You feel love for them. And, because of the love you have for them, you have courage enough to take them on.

Maria, Halle, and Mya—all teenage mothers—indicate strength and independence as constituents of womanhood. Like her schoolmates, Maria is also planning to graduate and to pursue college. However, unlike Halle and Mya, Maria's interpretation of what it means to be a woman is more explicitly articulated through her experience as a mother. In nearly every culture, motherhood precipitates womanhood by virtue of pregnancy and childbirth. For Maria, being a mother, and thusly a woman, is not just about having children, but also about possessing enough "love" and "courage" to be there for them, particularly when the father, according to Maria, may not be contributing adequate emotional or financial support.

From her comment, together with what the authors know about Maria's cultural background, it could be inferred that her maternal altruism is influenced by the cultural traditions of *familismo* (dispositions, values, and beliefs that place the welfare of the family first), as well as *marianismo* (women who self-deny and self-sacrifice for the good of the family). While these conventions might proffer insight into Maria's world, we believe that they cannot be used to wholly explicate her mind-set. Intracultural and individual variances in attitudes and behaviors within cultural groups must be considered, especially when attempting to decode the complexity of gender role expectations.

Individual variances aside, it is still essential to know how cultural systems and traditions work as they can influence personal decision making, which, in turn, affects community life. Presently, there is a substantial body of research that scrutinizes how and why Euro- and African-American girls accept or deny long-established gender expectations. As this literature grows, we still know little about the experiences of Mexican-American and Puerto Rican girls.

For example, how do they characterize femininity in relation to being Latina; what choices do they have in structuring their girlhood and womanhood; and, likewise, how do these alternatives manifest themselves in relationships and in their overall identity development? Given this query, we find that cultural systems have tremendous bearing on the lives of Latinas.

Familismo, regarded as one of the most significant cultural values among Hispanics, provides a network of social capital (family and peers) that has been known to generate a protective barrier against adverse experiences linked to minority status. Educational scholars assert that this network is responsible for high academic outcomes among Hispanic students. Other scholars, however, argue that *familismo* can lead some students to academically underperform, due to burdens and restrictions placed upon them by parents and extended family members.

Hispanic *familismo* (as with other forms of authoritarian, patriarchal structures within all cultures) renders a distinct set of conditions tied to gender expectations and sexual behavior. Anchored in Catholic principles, *familismo* produces a gender binary, characterizing men as masculine and dominant and women as feminine and submissive.

This cultural duality can push Latinas away from their academic and career goal attainment and more into traditional roles associated with child care and other domestic affairs. In a later segment of her interview, Maria confirmed this: "The only one that blocks my education is my boyfriend because he didn't want me to go to school. It's kind of chauvinist that 'you're the wife, you stay at home. You take care of the children and I graduate, and you're not graduating.'"

A 2009 report from the National Women's Law Center and Mexican American Legal Defense and Educational Fund found that one of the social barriers facing Chicana students is the task of caregiving for family members. The document claimed that Chicanas facing such responsibilities may be missing from school more regularly than their brothers, leading to academic dropout or disengagement.

The report further stated that strict family and societal gender expectations can engender feelings of low self-esteem among Latinas, especially if they see themselves in a substantively different light. For some ethnic minorities growing up in two cultures (e.g., Spanish and American), a level of tension can exist as they struggle with the expectations of their traditions versus the assimilating demands of mainstream society.

With respect to sexual behavior, Hispanic *familismo* regards the "ideal woman" to be one who represses her sexuality and defers to a man to teach her about it. In many Hispanic households, most notably those of Mexican immigrant and second-generation families, it is not uncommon for adolescent girls to engage in relationships with older men as there is familial acceptance toward teenage child-bearing.

Furthermore, religious values make conversations around sex and sexuality mute. Studies over the past several years have indicated that many Latinas do not have discussions with parents about sex or contraception. In fact, conservative Catholic teachings proclaim the use of birth control to be a sin. This belief, coupled with the manner in which the male-female binary is fulfilled, makes it improbable that contraception will be used.

The gender dynamics of *familismo* are necessary to understand as scholars believe that they play an essential part in high rates of Latina teenage motherhood. Briefly poring over national figures, between 1994 and 2006, Hispanic adolescents had the highest birth rate among the major ethnic groups. Though teenage pregnancy rates for Latinas have been dropping to some extent over the past twenty years, the reductions are not as sizable when matched against the numbers for non-Hispanic Whites.

Data from the Centers for Disease Control and Prevention's National Center for Health Statistics showed that the 2007 birth rate among Latinas ages fifteen to nineteen was at 81.7 per 1,000; Blacks in the same age bracket were at 64.3 per 1,000; and non-Hispanic Whites were at 27.2 per 1,000. While examining the disparity in the above ratios is crucial, the consequences of teenage pregnancy for Latinas, as well as *all* girls, are also necessary to be aware of. Adolescent mothers can be subjected to a level of physical and psychological stress that stems not only from pregnancy, but also from an overload of motherhood responsibilities.

Studies have reported that the unmarried high school mom is twice as likely as her peers to drop out, forgo college, and earn less money. There is also the decreased likelihood that many of the fathers, particularly fathers of color, will gain access to sustained employment and be able to consistently support their child. Furthermore, children born to teen mothers, particularly from low socioeconomic communities, are more likely to have academic and behavioral problems, are more susceptible to health issues, and run a greater risk of enduring economic poverty.

Latinas are not beyond these circumstances. Approximately 69 percent of Hispanic mothers abandon high school compared to 58 percent of teenage mothers overall. In 2005, less than 60 percent of Hispanic adults in the U.S. earned a high school diploma as more than one in five was living beneath the poverty line. Sadly, 30 percent of all children living in poverty are Latino.

Even though researchers draw a compelling relationship between Hispanic *familismo* and teenage pregnancy and the dropout rate, we must realize that a successful future is not lost on adolescent Latina mothers. For one thing, some schools offer these students assistance by way of tutoring, counseling, mentoring, and even free day care. Such programs are indispensable as they keep young moms near to their academic goals and prevent them from dropping off the radar screen.

Also, despite the patriarchal undercurrent running through *familismo*, it can provide a level of support by way of family and peer networks concerned with educational success, job attainment, and emotional well-being. This form of social cohesiveness is central for young pregnant Latinas who are still maturing socially and emotionally and who may also become isolated in schools and in peer circles due to their pregnancy.

By examining the influence of Hispanic *familismo* closer, we can (as with any other cultural system) broaden our understanding as to why personal decisions are made and how such choices affect families. Moreover, we can extend our awareness of how different Latinas navigate relationships across home and community spaces, rather than relying upon blanketing cultural assumptions to help explain their respective lives. Though Maria may be influenced (consciously or unconsciously) by cultural traditions, she demonstrates a level of equanimity between school and maternal demands. This is evidenced by her conviction to stay with her education, in spite of what social conventions obligate her to do.

Nikki

Nikki is seventeen, African-American, and lives with foster parents. She experienced a turbulent childhood and still copes with issues as an adolescent. She describes herself as "strong-willed, worthy, and someone trying every day to master peace." Nikki wants to graduate in the following school year and become a singer and motivational speaker. She says that she is a spiritual person and seeks to "inspire others through words and song." When Nikki sings, the moving tenor of her voice reveals her life, her dreams, and the power of her faith.

> Women struggle. But, as a woman, even though you struggle, you have to be a conqueror. You have to go forward, even though you got something that's hard in your life. You have to be able to move forward and kick the bricks when you got to. You're strong, you can make it through situations, you're confident in things. Even when you going through something, you don't have to do it by yourself. You can reach out for help.

In addition to being a returning student, Nikki also lives in foster care and faces many social and emotional difficulties. In spite of this, she affirms herself as "strong-willed and worthy." As the authors are unaware of her specific experiences growing up in both foster care and group homes, to say that her seventeen-year journey has been less than daunting would be a miscalculation. We do know, however, that some of Nikki's experiences mirror those of other young people who have been shuffled in and out of the foster care system.

Presently in the U.S. there are over half a million children living in foster care. Data from the Adoption and Foster Care Analysis and Reporting System (AFCARS) reported that in 2006, of the estimated 303,000 children who entered foster care, White youth constituted 45 percent; African-Americans were at 26 percent; Hispanics at 19 percent; and "other races or multiracial" were listed at 10 percent.

Regarding youth of color, additional studies on foster care cite that Hispanic children are placed at younger ages and for longer periods than White youth. Black children receive fewer services than Whites and continue in placement longer. The latter helps to explain the disproportionate overrepre-

sentation of African-Americans in the system. For both groups, there is limited research on service utilization and developmental outcomes.

For youth in foster care, developmental changes can be complicated by a
host of factors—limited financial support and resources; a history of family
abuse and neglect; frequent moving from one living condition to another;
low self-esteem; minimal educational success; addiction and mental health
issues; court involvement; and fear of disclosing their backgrounds as they
chance being stigmatized by child welfare workers, teachers, and schoolmates.

For girls, the distress of sharing their histories is intensified if they have
suffered sexual violence at the hands of peers and adults—some of whom are
family members. Currently, there is vast paucity in qualitative research that
investigates the experiences of girls of color living in foster care. Existent
studies typically amass girls into a singular class category, with little attention paid to race and ethnicity. Even so, these reports offer significant information on the specific problems facing these young people.

Beyond those factors listed above, other studies report that girls are at
greater odds of early pregnancy and parenthood, either while being in the
system or after transitioning out of it. The National Campaign to Prevent
Teen Pregnancy conducted a study in 2006, documenting that 33 percent of
girls in foster care had been pregnant at least one time by the age of seventeen and 71 percent by the age of twenty-one.

The National Campaign to Prevent Teen and Unplanned Pregnancy found
that adolescent girls in the system are 2.5 times more likely to get pregnant
by age nineteen than peers not in foster care.[6] Although becoming a parent
can further destabilize girls' lives, additional systems such as *supportive
housing* offer adolescent parents a safe place to live with child care, voca-
tional training, and physical and mental health services.

Given the various hardships that Nikki faces in her life, she does not have
to deal with the added pressure of being a teen parent. Her approach to
everyday stress is found in her interpretation of womanhood, proclaiming
that a woman must "be able to move forward and kick the bricks." She goes
on to add, "Even though you struggle, you have to be a conqueror. . . . You're
strong, you can make it through situations, you're confident in things." The
authors situate Nikki's comments within the framework of *Black womanhood*.

Scholars have contended that, for some African-American women, the
shared traits of assertiveness, self-determination, fortitude, and resistance
emerge out of a history of racial oppression. Beginning as early as U.S.
slavery, Black women were forced to operate in similar roles as their Black
male counterparts, assuming tasks that demanded initiative and self-reliance.
During slavery, African-American female consignment radically differed

from Euro-American conceptions of womanhood, which relegated White women to passive and subordinate statuses.

As previously stated, Black women, historically and up to the present, have always performed in the multiple capacities of mother, worker, and provider. The strengths (e.g., persistence, ingenuity, resilience) that African-American girls exhibit are thought to derive from familial and nonfamilial women—mothers, grandmothers, aunts, teachers, and mentors—passing down life lessons. These intergenerational cues function as a protective barrier against a society long regarded by African-Americans as prejudiced toward Black identities—female and male.

Regrettably, the "inherited" attributes of Black girls are often interpreted (against the backdrop of conventional femininity) as obstinate, aggressive, and disobedient behaviors. Society's knee-jerk response to such conduct has been to silence and sanction females of color through school suspensions, expulsions, and, in other cases, detention and incarceration. These punishments can certainly whittle away at a resilient veneer.

As opposed to rushed discipline, we must first reflect on and look deeper into the source of the behavior that we have construed as insubordinate and unacceptable. When working alongside young females of color, particularly those who are experiencing difficult times and are hard to reach, we must be conscious of and act against traditional societal norms, as well as public rhetoric, that misrepresent this social group. Without doing so, we will be ineffective in supplying these young people with genuine forms of outreach that speak to *their* immediate conditions, as well as *their* future aspirations.

Nikki believes, in spite of her struggles, that young women confronting adversity are not alone, that they can "reach out for help." For the authors, providing girls of color from disadvantaged communities with greater access to compassionate and caring adults is an urgent issue that must be addressed concurrently in and outside of schools. In later sections of this book, we discuss the responsibility of teachers, principals, mentors, and parents in answering the needs of adolescent girls of color.

CLOSING COMMENTS AND RECOMMENDED RESOURCES

The odds stacked against the young women above are undeniably profound. To suggest that all youth of color from disadvantaged communities will be able to transcend a life of poverty in American society, would be unrealistic. Nonetheless, in reaching out to underprivileged youth, we cannot waver in our efforts to authentically engage them in high levels of intervention, access, and equity. This calls for us, in part, to continue to question and demand the accountability of social institutions that purposely or not function to restrict the life options of these youngsters.

With respect to teenage pregnancy, girls and young women of color encounter a range of societal responses around motherhood. Within a larger social context, some are perceived as "bad girls" because of their young age and loss of childhood innocence. In their respective communities, these girls and young women, while disdained by some, are seen by others as achieving a status and rite of passage into adulthood. The fact that some females of color persist with schooling and employment is a strong indicator of the resilience and personal power that they possess.

In any case, we must pay more attention to why girls become pregnant before finishing school or gaining financial independence and viability. The idea that some become pregnant as a means of healing their childhood scars and achieving a closeness and support that they could not find in the home is troubling at least. Below is an assortment of resources related to many of the topics undertaken in this chapter. Educators and youth workers may find the following beneficial in augmenting their practice, while girls and young women may find these sources helpful in their future decision making.

Books

Against Machismo: Young Adult Voices in Mexico City by José Ramirez (2008/Berghahn Publishers).

Black Women, Identity, and Cultural Theory: Unbecoming the Subject by Kevin Everod Quashie (2004/Rutgers University Press).

Foster Care Odyssey: A Black Girl's Story by Theresa Cameron (2002/University Press of Mississippi).

Gather Together in My Name by Maya Angelou (1985/Bentham Publishers).

GirlSource: A Book by and for Young Women about Relationships, Rights, Futures, Bodies, Minds, and Souls by the GirlSource editorial team: Jessica Barnes and others (2003/Ten Speed Press).

The Machismo and Marianismo Tango by David Sequeira (2009/Dorrance Publishing Co.).

Pregnant Bodies, Fertile Minds: Gender, Race, and the Schooling of Pregnant Teens by Wendy Luttrell (2003/Routledge Press).

The Underground Guide to Teenage Sexuality, 2nd Edition by Michael J. Basso (2003/Fairview Press).

Articles

The "batty" politic: Toward an aesthetic of the Black female body by Janell Hobson (2003/*Hypatia* 18(4): 87–105).

Black adolescent racial identity and respectability by Garrett Albert Duncan and Henrika McCoy (2007/*Negro Educational Review* 58(1–2): 35–48).

Gender socialization in Latino/a families: Results from two retrospective studies by Marcela Raffaelli and Lenna L. Ontai (2004/*Sex Roles* 50(5/6): 287–299).

Masculine femininities/feminine masculinities: Power, identities and gender by Carrie Paechter (2006/*Educational Studies* 18(3): 253–263).

Reconciling messages: The process of sexual talk for Latinas by Sandra Faulkner and Phyllis Kernoff Mansfield (2002/*Qualitative Health Research* 12: 310–328).

The transformation of girls to women: Finding voice and developing strategies for liberation by Elizabeth Iglesias and Sherry Cormier (2002/*Journal of Multicultural Counseling and Development* 30(4): 259–71).

Websites and Organizations

The Beehive (www.beehive.org) provides a thorough listing of national scholarships and grants available for minority students and adolescent mothers.

Chicago Child Care Society (cccsociety.org) serves vulnerable children and their families in the Chicago, Illinois, area.

Child Care Association of Illinois (cca-il.org) works with neglected and abused children and their families. Also provides services that include foster care, residential care, and in-home support services.

Federal Supplemental Educational Opportunity Grant (www.ed.gov) program offers grants to low-income undergraduate students seeking to continue their education at a postsecondary institution.

Healthy Teen Network (www.healthyteennetwork.org), located in Baltimore, Maryland, is a national resource for professionals whose practice focuses on teenage pregnancy, prevention, and parenting.

1. Even though early identity theories on adolescence provide key insights into the psychological domain of young people, much of these works are based on White, middle-class males and imbued with monocultural notions of autonomy, independence, and separation. Missing from most traditional interpretations of identity formation are the experiences of women and people of color. For more female-oriented theories, we can turn to the work of Carol Gilligan and Ruthellan Josselson—scholars who highlight the importance of relatedness and attachment in women's lives. For theories centered on racial identity development, we can look to the work of William Cross, Janet Helms, and Beverly D. Tatum.

2. Historically and presently, the message of "masculine as provider" has not been a role that some Black men have been able to fulfill due to a history of slavery, institutionalized racism, and high rates of unemployment and underemployment. In turn, Black males more readily adopt the singular message of "masculine as dominant," which creates a set of language and behaviors typified by aggression, toughness, power, and even violence—attributes that, while working to safeguard their manhood, function to mask pain, doubt, fear, and adversity.

3. In 2009, teenage pregnancy rates among Chicago Public School (CPS) students were nearly at 13 percent. At Paul Robeson High School, for example, 115 out of 800 students were pregnant in 2009. The 13 percent pregnancy figure is an interesting statistic given that CPS's student body is roughly 85 percent Black and Hispanic.

4. Data from 2008–2009 from four-year college institutions show that the disparity in the number of Hispanic and White college students who graduate with a bachelor's degree is wider than the gap in high school completion rates. Data from four-year institutions also report that only 46 percent of Black students, 47 percent of Hispanic students, and 54 percent of low-income students graduate within six years. While women of color have outpaced their male counterparts in both college matriculation and graduation, their numbers still remain far lower than White females.

5. West Stevens, J. (2002). *Smart and Sassy: The Inner Strengths of Inner-City Black Girl.* New York: Oxford University Press.

6. It should be noted that teen pregnancy and parenthood in foster care is not necessarily a by-product of being in the system. In most cases, it is children's prior exposure to risky behaviors that precede their placement, being that a majority of them are victims of abandonment, as well as sexual and physical abuse.

Chapter Two

Is It Real or Is It Media?

The emotional, sexual, and psychological stereotyping of females begins when the doctor says, "It's a girl." —*Shirley Chisholm*

No matter what a woman's appearance may be, it will be used to undermine what she is saying and taken to individualize—as her personal problem—observations she makes about the beauty myth in society. —*Naomi Wolf*

Media comprises newspapers, magazines and books, movies, television, radio, and the Internet. Together, these various forms of communication make up one of the most influential forces in our present world. Media, particularly television and the Internet, offers us virtually unlimited access to news and events occurring globally. This access, of sound and imagery, plays an active role in how we see the world and interact within it.

Young people, most notably, have been the center of much attention with regard to the effects of media on their everyday life. Voluminous amounts of research over the past few decades claim that media programming serves as a kind of curriculum that shapes young people's behavior and informs them about values. Although some claim that media engages young people in healthy and productive ways, there are those who insist that its effects are damaging to both youth and society.

With reference to its positive influences, mass media facilitates social awareness for youth, providing information on an array of subject matter that may not be addressed in either schools or homes (e.g., health care, unemployment rates, child labor, global poverty, and homelessness). Additionally, studies have also noted that assorted forms of media promote literacy through the analysis and evaluation of its messages.

Conversely, the adverse effects of mass media on young people have been far more documented. Much of the public concern has revolved around the impression that media images and messages have on children and adolescents, negatively altering their perceptions of behavior, body image, and sexuality. In fact, parents and professionals alike have made direct correlations between media exposure, youth violence, and sexual activity. Societal responses to the harmful impact of media have included policy interventions in the form of parental warning labels on audio CDs with explicit lyrics, as well as the passage of the Telecommunications Act of 1996.[1]

In spite of the larger, public debate around media, it does have specific purposes for adolescents. Developmental psychologist, Jeffrey Jansen Arnett,[2] proposes that, for teenagers, media has five major functions: entertainment, high sensation, coping, youth culture identification, and identity formation.

Movies, television, music, and video games, for instance, represent enormous sources of entertainment for young people. These media outlets can be enjoyed with family or peers or in isolation. Likewise, these same outlets enhance and broaden young people's sensory experience through visual imagery and sound. An action film or a booming hip-hop song can offer a person intense sensory stimulation.

Young people further consume different types of media to help cope with personal feelings. "Adolescents use media to relieve and dispel negative emotions. Several studies indicate that 'Listen to music' and 'Watch TV' are the coping strategies most commonly used by adolescents when they are angry, anxious, or unhappy" (Arnett 1995, 523). In their quest for social recognition, teens also make use of mass media to enhance their "sense of being connected to youth culture or subculture" (524). Following trends or "fitting in" is important for some teenagers as it grants them entrée and membership into the peer group.

"Being connected" ties in with Arnett's last function of media, as young people further utilize it to help resolve questions around identity. In mediating their personality, interests, and abilities, adolescents often search for images that reflect who they are or desire to be. The comparisons they find not only inform them about behavior, morality, and relationships, but also become yardsticks for self-evaluation.

For better or for worse, media is a major force in the lives of adolescents. There is no question that it is a curriculum that socializes and works to shape young people's worldview—how they perceive themselves and subsequently relate to others. Over the past three decades, one of the more influential media forms has been music videos. This medium has proven to be a dynamic venue for pop and hip-hop culture, and arguably has become more influential than radio. Some artists utilize music videos as a tool to create distinct images for their songs, inviting viewers into their interpretation of the lyrics. Yet, some argue that far too many artists, specifically of hip-hop, are making videos that venerate sex and wealth.

One problem this presents is that such videos narrowly define for young people the way in which material assets are achieved. Instead, viewers are enticed with sparkling affluence and gleaming status. Yet, who could blame them? They see all of the accoutrements and trademarks that come with such standing and want a slice of the proverbial pie.

Another problem posed by hip-hop videos is the way in which women of color are represented. Absent, for the most part, are healthy, constructive images of Black and Hispanic females. Some scholars argue that when youngsters view images of half-naked women dancing seductively, the implication is that their female minds are unnecessary and that their bodies are commodities. The body, in many respects, becomes a bargaining chip that girls and young women can trade or sell for attention and financial gain.

Other scholars point out that such imagery illustrates women of color as hypersexual and promiscuous—neither being cultural norms for African-American and Hispanic women. In fact, research on the sexual behavior of women of color report that they are more likely to be in monogamous relationships that mimic marriage. Certainly, pop and hip-hop videos are not the principal force behind sexism or racism. They are, however, works that often represent deeply embedded values of a patriarchal society—a powerful agent in how Latinas and African-American females are socialized.

Given this argument, several questions arise: How do adolescents either resist or resign to media as a curriculum; how are females of color constructed by mainstream ideals and standards embodied in media programming; and how do they respond to media representations of their race, ethnicity, class, and gender? To help address this query, we asked a few of our participants their opinion on mass media—mainly television and music videos.

STEREOTYPES AND BODY POLITICS

Lapita

Society thinks that whatever we see on TV, of course, we gonna wind up trying to do, and sometimes that's true. Like all these videos about money, bling-bling, and all these guys with cars, everybody wants to be doing that. Even when videos talk about shooting somebody, when you go out and try to do it, it's not that easy. You're going get caught, if you're not smart. You like a certain video, so you do what you see. But whatever you see on TV you ain't necessarily gotta do. I don't follow stuff because of a video.

Lapita was first introduced in chapter 1, offering her stance on the difference between girlhood and womanhood. Here, she discusses the weight of media, as a curriculum, and how youth model its content. While Lapita admits that young people "sometimes" replicate behaviors found within music videos, she also claims that she is able to discriminate between such material and reality. This juxtaposition resonates with two opposing viewpoints relative to mass media exposure: 1) the largely held argument that media negatively shapes youngsters' perceptions and behavior; and 2) the lesser explored notion that youth possess certain capacities that enable them to detach from media inducements and not replicate its content.

Concerning the first point, Lapita states: "Like all these videos about money, bling-bling, and all these guys with cars, everybody wants to be doing that. . . . You like a certain video, so you do what you see." For the authors, this remark is consistent with *Social Learning Theory*. Initially developed by psychologist Albert Bandura, this seminal work posits that human behavior is mostly learned through observation. By watching others, people generate new ideas around conduct, which serves as information for later possible action.

Over the past forty years, *Social Learning Theory* has served as the basis for hundreds of studies focused on the effects of media on children and adolescents. These studies report, for instance, that recurring exposure to erotic content can prompt young people to experiment with sexual acts at younger ages. Short- and long-term contact with violent images is also believed to increase the likelihood that youth will be verbally and physically hostile.

Equal to its capabilities in eliciting aggressive behavior, other studies have shown that media violence often portrays the world as an unsafe place, generating extreme panic and fear in both children and adolescents. In keeping with *Social Learning Theory*, the environment not only causes our behavior, but our behavior also causes the environment. Thus, extreme violent acts initially seen on TV, and then later carried out, can engender feelings of hostility and anxiety among individuals in social settings, without them ever being exposed to the original media source.

Although media retains a profound socializing element, it does not have total power and control over how young people think and develop. Lapita states it plainly: "But whatever you see on TV you ain't necessarily gotta do. I don't follow stuff because of a video." This comment lends itself to those internal and external factors that play a role in how Lapita, and other adolescents, might counter media socialization.

First, an individual's own unique temperament determines, in part, how they respond to sensory cues from mass media or other environmental sources. A child, for example, watching a violent television show might react immediately by copying the observed behavior. Another child, viewing the same program, may perceive the images as brutal, upsetting, or unrealistic, and choose not to emulate the event. Hence, how one assesses surrounding stimuli, in this case TV violence, to some measure, depends on one's innate way of interrelating with the world.

A second factor integral to young folks' capacity to separate media content from reality is their cognitive development. With the adolescent mind becoming progressively more analytical, two fundamental skill sets emerge: *decision making* and *critical thinking*. As such, youth now begin monitoring their own thoughts and making judgments about societal rules, institutional values, and group morals. Through critical thinking and decision making, youth are able to make self-evaluations about what is valid or invalid, agreeable or disagreeable, in mass media themes.

The expanding adolescent mind helps to render the third and final factor in young people's ability to judge media programming. In light of their burgeoning conceptual thoughts, teenagers are more readily able to engage in critical dialogue around what they see and listen to. This is a time when educators and other adults can assist adolescents in better understanding the subject matter that they are being exposed to.

Educational scholars have noted that involving students in critiques of media increases their comprehension of how it works, how it is organized, its multiple meanings, and how reality can be constructed through its transmission. Too often, educators feel that it is inappropriate or distracting to examine media as curricular content and thus ignore its potential utility.

In her article "The Body of Evidence: Dangerous Intersections between Development and Culture in the Lives of Adolescent Girls,"[3] Mary K. Bentley writes:

> All youth need to learn to critique the messages that inundate them by measuring these messages against their lived experiences, not the "real" as depicted by television, advertisements, magazines, and mannequins. This kind of vigilance gives girls a tool, a way to sift through the images and messages, and make meaning of them in a conscious way. (219)

Without critical examination of media content, Bentley argues that girls and young women can develop self-defeating behaviors that culminate in outward expressions of anger or internalized feelings of extreme pain.

Mira

Mira is African-American, seventeen years of age, and a mother of one. She describes herself as "beautiful and intelligent, but mean." She enjoys school-club activities and hanging out with her friends and boyfriend. After graduating, she plans to continue her education by going to college. Mira states that she wants to become a doctor and raise her daughter "the best way possible." At the start of her group interview, Mira was quiet, appearing slightly disinterested in the process. With her peers engaged and sharing their opinions, Mira began gradually opening up and adding to the conversation.

> Black and Hispanic girls are stereotyped on TV as being little hos and being hot. They say we get pregnant at a young age. They say we ghetto, we can't talk, we not educated, stuff like that. But we break those stereotypes by showing them, by staying in school, being educated, being a doctor or lawyer. But if you do get pregnant at a young age, you still keep going. You don't stop.

Shanny

Shanny is eighteen and African-American. She describes herself as "a cheerful Aquarius" who "parties responsibly." She likes to shop and to be with her family. Shanny's goals, after finishing high school, include buying a car and going to college to study accounting.

> People say that the videos we make these days show women disrespecting ourselves. We have no type of femininity and we just out there. It's just like a Nelly video—you see this young Black woman shaking her butt in front of the television naked. They'll say that she's probably a slut, or a ho, or a tramp just because she did something to make some money. But she probably didn't do it just to be in the video. She probably had to make the money that she needed. Now, my young niece loves watching videos. She tries to do everything she sees in them. But, it's like, sometimes I have to sit her down and let her know that this is not reality, that it's only TV.

Like Lapita, Mira and Shanny both exhibit an awareness of the socializing power of media, as well as a level of opposition to it. Mira and Shanny, however, give a more exact perspective on media depictions of women of color. For the authors, both student comments evoke the theory of *sexual scripts*. Fundamental to gender socialization, these schematic cues are conveyed through the environment (vis-à-vis messages and social interactions), informing individuals as to what is appropriate and expected in sexual situations.

For example, in American society, sexual scripts for males frequently convey sex as something entertaining, leisurely, or only for physical gratification. Alternatively, for females, sexual scripts tend to structure sexuality as something to be explored for the purpose of relational or psychological intimacy (i.e., romance). The manner in which an individual organizes sexual schema, and then develops sexual attitudes and behaviors, becomes part and parcel of how one sees oneself as a sexual being and how others might perceive him or her in the same way.

For females of color, sexual scripts are deeply rooted in a cultural context. In Latin communities, for instance, male dominance can produce weighty expectations for Latinas to engage in sexual intercourse with a love interest.

This is seen as permissible if the relationship is exclusively long-standing, monogamous, and heterosexual. Adolescent Latinas can still be perceived as good girls if the sexual activity, either forced or permitted, is founded on the mutual feeling of "being in love."

It should be noted that sexual activity for Latinas can also be a confusing experience as the culture of *machismo* expects girls to be virginal, while at the same time compliant to the needs and desires of the male. Those Latinas deviating from this male-centered standard (e.g., having more than one partner, being homosexual, or taking on more mainstream ideals of relationships) run the risk of being harassed, alienated, or isolated by others.

Ideas on love and sexuality for African-American girls emerge largely out of mainstream societal behaviors. Like most teens, African-American females can also be found dating and involved in mate selections based on romantic ideals of love. Unfortunately, this cultural group is frequently stereotyped as being more sexually involved than their White counterparts. This generalization upholds the myth that teenage pregnancy is more socially acceptable in the Black community.

Sexual scripts for African-American women in particular have been distinctively framed by a plethora of images: the subservient and asexual Mammy; the innately libidinous Jezebel; the Welfare-reliant Baby's Mamma; the scantily dressed and oversexualized Video Vixen; and most recently, the brassy Diva and money-hungry Gold Digger. Largely promulgated through mass media, these crude and oversimplified depictions, in one sense, project narrow scripts of what it means to be Black, female, and sexual. In another sense, they blatantly indicate the value that American society has placed upon Black women overall.

So how do gender and racial stereotypes affect the young women represented here? Bearing in mind our previous discussion on adolescent responses to mass media programming, individual reactions can manifest themselves in any number of ways. In Mira's case, television stereotypes of females of color should be broken and not followed. She claims, "We break those stereotypes by showing them, by staying in school, being educated, being a doctor or lawyer."

Mira's strong resistance to stereotypes may very well be fueled by her presently strong focus on life goals. However, in her defiance, she is also exerting a level of personal agency that redefines culturally based sexual scripts that have been legitimated and normalized through mass media and society. Mira, in effect, is aware of gender and racial stereotypes surrounding African-American and Latina females, but chooses not to fit within these sexual consignments.

Her reaction reinforces the notion that adolescents possess the power to either accept or reject societal scripts and, in the process, develop their own unique identity and perspective. It also suggests that it is vastly important for some students of color to resist artificially constructed images, as these representations simply do not resonate with who they are or desire to be.

Even though Mira has a child, she remains adamant: "If you do get pregnant at a young age, you still keep going. You don't stop." Here, we observe Mira's resistance to being pigeonholed as the sexually configured Baby's Mamma. Moreover, we also detect her resilience in refuting this blanket imagery through her motivation in bettering her life and the life of her child by means of education.

Shanny is also challenging media programming as exemplified in her statement about her niece: "She tries to do everything she sees in them. . . . sometimes I have to sit her down and let her know that this is not reality, that it's only TV." Her ability to separate media content from reality surely derives from her level of maturity and life experiences.

Her opposition to music video stereotypes, however, is not a total refutation of them, but rather a deeper analysis of the imagery itself. In her response, Shanny questions those labels recurrently attached to Video Vixens and proposes a rationale as to why these women participate in such work: "They'll say that she's probably a slut, or a ho, or a tramp just because she did something to make some money. But she probably didn't do it just to be in the video. She probably had to make the money that she needed."

It might be fair to conclude, from her interpretation, that Shanny is able to effectively problematize institutional values and norms. Through her own evaluation, she has determined what is valid or invalid with regard to how sexual scripts limit and objectify women of color. Shanny is indeed adding dimension, context, and humanness to the regularly perceived one-dimensional representation of the Video Vixen. While such mediation may speak to her own personal agency, it may also be a product of her ability to critically articulate and share her thoughts on the implicit and explicit messages found in music videos.

An added aspect of media stereotypes, which is also implied in Shanny's response, is how social class is portrayed, particularly when fused with race and gender. While media representations of sex and violence are widely considered as two major elements that negatively influence young people's attitude and conduct, another facet of media socialization garnering little attention is class status.

Rarely are depictions of class deemed a variable in adolescent identity development. In other words, how do young people evaluate themselves, if at all, when faced with positive or negative depictions of their class affiliation? In Mira's response above, she mentions how Black and Latina girls are stereotyped as "ghetto" and "uneducated," which denotes a lower class. Such characterizations for African-American women are, once again, personified in the Brassy Diva and Baby's Mamma caricatures.

For Latinas, mass media consistently portrays them as sexual and foreign. Although the Hispanic community has received increased exposure in recent years, illuminating rich and contextual multiple cultures, mainstream television and films still widely depict Spanish characters as poor, lazy, clownish, uneducated, and violent. Like many of the stereotypical minor roles that feature African-Americans, Hispanics have also been relegated to such characters as landscaper, janitor, gangbanger, cook, or teenage mother. It is in these parts that we also interestingly find inverted gender scripts that present men as childlike and droll and women as more reasonable and intelligent than males.

Irrespective of one's class, such images can leave scathing impressions on how individuals within these cultures perceive themselves, as well as how they are treated by others in or outside of their ethnic group. Later, in chapter 5, we look more closely at the school domain and the effect that social class and racial stereotypes have on teacher-student relationships.

Concerning mass media and gender socialization overall, we live in a society obsessed with the corporeal. Teen magazines strongly focus on beauty, fashion, weight, and sexual attractiveness toward males. Television, like such magazines, constantly displays images of the "perfect girl" as sweet and dainty, with smooth skin and a permanent smile. The visuals, by and large, do very little to represent the multiple dimensions of girls and women. Instead, we are left with skewed conceptions of "girlness"—ones that are vacuous and objectifying.

For African-American and Hispanic females, the vast majority of this imagery reflects standards of beauty that run counter to their own cultural frames of reference. If beauty has been traditionally defined by Eurocentric yardsticks, then how do women of color measure up in comparison? The consequences of these standards are tragic at best. These women find themselves obsessed with physical traits that they can never naturally achieve—fair skin; blue eyes; straight, blond hair; thin lips and nose; and narrow, slender hips. Such attributes are generally not the norm in African-American or Hispanic communities.

While there are cosmetic procedures that allow ethnic women to attain this kind of beauty, what expense does it pose to their bodies and to their self-esteem? In spite of the politics of phenotype that create unhealthy affinities for Eurocentric characteristics and images, there are some nontraditional forms of beauty among African-American and Latina women that seem to be acceptable in mainstream culture.

Representations of Black and Hispanic women are largely characterized by an emphasis on the breasts, hips, and buttocks. Salma Hayek, Beyoncé Knowles, and Jennifer Lopez provide intriguing examples of the fixation with the stereotype of women of color with curves and a large backside. In

2004, scores of plastic surgeons reported a surge of interest in implants that would make women look more like these Hollywood stars.

Recently, less drastic methods for attaining the "hourglass shape" have included undergarments that raise and accentuate a woman's buttocks. Because a little "junk in the trunk" became en vogue, what was previously forbidden became sexy and "acceptable." Ironically, many African-American and Hispanic girls, who are naturally stout, chunky, or "pleasantly plump," see the curvaceous body type as equally unachievable as the Euro-centric waiflike one.

A large segment of research has been devoted to how teenage girls deal with body development during puberty. Most of this inquiry has centered on the experiences of Euro-American girls and the current societal expectations around the ultra-thin female body. Consistent research findings point to the pressures that many White girls feel to conform to this "ideal" image, as well as the deleterious strategies they perform in trying to achieve it—overexercising and extreme diets. These measures have been highly documented as leading to such outcomes as low self-esteem, depression, as well as eating disorders (e.g., anorexia and bulimia nervosa).

Some African-American and Hispanic girls are alternatively impacted by a different set of cultural influences. These girls and young women place a higher value on a larger, more voluptuous female body and less often perceive themselves as overweight compared to White females. In some cases, the heavier body type is viewed not only as more physically attractive to males, but also as reflecting a strong, well-nourished individual. Often attached to these cultural referents of body image is the stigma that girls of color are more likely to suffer from obesity than White girls.

In a 2004 report by the Girls Scouts of the USA, one in five Latinas was assessed as overweight. These girls were also deemed as being the least physically active of all female cultural groups. Even as they were evaluated as overweight by mainstream standards, the participants attested to feeling secure with their bodies. One correlated finding in their positive perception was that nine out of ten mothers of these "overweight" girls frequently made constructive comments about their daughters' body. In other words, these young Latinas received positive reinforcement relative to their exterior, which contradicts Western society's endorsement of the need to be thin.

Even with African-American and Latina groups' support of the curvy, full-figured body, we are witnessing increasing numbers of young women of color struggling with body dissatisfaction issues that lead to eating disorders like anorexia and bulimia nervosa. Though widely regarded as a White female phenomenon, recent studies have shown that Black and Hispanic females are at equal risk or higher for developing these addictions.

A 2003 study by *American Journal of Psychiatry* revealed that African-American women were just as likely White women to report binge eating or vomiting, with Black women more likely to self-report fasting and the use of laxatives. The *Journal of Medicine and Health* reported in 2009 that Black teenage girls were 50 percent more likely than their white counterparts to demonstrate bulimic behavior, including overeating and purging.

Data on eating illnesses among U.S. Latinas is greatly limited. Researchers, however, believe that acculturation into mainstream society pushes some Hispanic women away from traditional aesthetic values and expectations, leaving them at greater risk for developing disorders. Further, Latinas of higher socioeconomic status have been found to be more at risk for eating pathologies over lower socioeconomic Latinas, with social mobility being a sharp indicator of increased assimilation.

For both groups, there is still very little supportive evidence as to why they experience bulimia or anorexia. This is partly due to the fallacy that these syndromes are a "White woman's disease." This misconception has led to not only inadequate research on ethnic groups and eating syndromes, but also the improbability that a clinician will diagnosis a person of color as having one, much less a person of color reporting and receiving treatment for one.

Regardless of the misperceptions around eating disorders and who can have one and who cannot, one requisite in the development of these pathologies, despite race, class, or gender, is low self-esteem. Our attitudes about ourselves are closely tied with body image. For teens and young adults, low self-esteem can engender distorted perceptions about one's body and self-worth. In order to fully change one's negative self-perception, self-esteem issues must first be dealt with.

As parents, educators, and anyone working with young people, it is critical not to ignore those conflicting messages that *every* girl receives about her body. For young women of color, this becomes paramount as they, in many ways, can look considerably different from conventional Western standards of beauty. In a society that associates being thin with being feminine, it is imperative that we create spaces for females of color to discuss, interrogate, and challenge images of what women should look like and who they should be.

CLOSING COMMENTS AND RECOMMENDED RESOURCES

The physical growth that accompanies puberty has many of our adolescents looking and feeling like early adults. When some young people are developing ahead of their peers, their bodily changes can mislead them in thinking they are socially and emotionally ready for adult life. Likewise, adults can also be misguided in thinking that young people's minds and emotional states are as equally as developed as their bodies.

The physically developed girl as emotionally mature is unquestionably a falsehood. Even though Black and Hispanic adolescent females may display an adult body, we find very little parity with this and their emotional side. Indeed, we must peer beyond the corporeal and explore other dimensions that these young women hold of value (e.g., personal competencies, sense of purpose, intellect, and spirituality).

On another note, yet related to external appearances, African-American, Chicana, and Puerto Rican females are inundated by media images that positively and negatively portray their race, ethnicity, class, and gender. Some females, like our participants above, are able to filter through these differences and draw on what they need, while others may not be readily able to do so.

Media images, and the curriculum of these images, operate as a vehicle for transmitting the codes and traditions of mainstream society. Representations of race and gender are so intensely engrained into our psyches that we often fail to see them as biased and legitimized constructions of knowledge that position women and ethnic groups as "other."

The adolescent mind is more than capable of probing curriculum (e.g., films, books, newspapers, magazines, songs) that transmits ideologies of power and unequal social relations. Thus, teachers at middle- and high-school levels can employ critical literacy methods that will encourage girls of color to question societal institutions and practices that are normalized, but not experienced by all members of society.

Such lessons might find students critiquing phenomenon like the politics of the human body, sexuality, femininity, masculinity, culture, family, poverty, equity, and justice. Below is a list of resources related to critical literacy, as well as other topics, discussed in this chapter.

Books

Critical Literacy/Critical Teaching: Tools for Preparing Responsive Teachers by Cheryl Dozier, Peter Johnston, and Rebecca Rogers (2006/Teachers College Press).

Critical Literacy and Urban Youth: Pedagogies of Access, Dissent, and Liberation by Ernest Morrell (2007/Routledge Publishers).

Gaining: The Truth About Life After Eating Disorders by Aimee Liu (2007/Warner Books).

Girls in Real Life Situations, Grades 6–12: Group Counseling Activities for Enhancing Social and Emotional Development by Julia V. Taylor and Shannon Trice-Black (2010/Research Press).

Hungry for More: A Keeping-it-Real Guide for Black Women on Weight and Body Image by Robyn McGee (2005/Seal Press).

Latina Teens, Migration, and Popular Culture by Lucila Vargas (2009/Peter Lang Publishing).

Not All Black Girls Know How to Eat: A Story of Bulimia by Stephanie Covington Armstrong (2009/Lawrence Hill Books).

Velvet Barrios: Popular Culture & Chicana/o Sexualities by Alicia Gaspar de Alba and Tomas Ybarra Frausto (2003/Palgrave-Macmillan Publishers).

Why We Hate Black Women: Deconstructing the Paradox of Black Female Masculinity by Hasani Pettiford (2010/Blue Magic Publishing).

Articles

Adolescent Latinas' adaptive functioning and sense of well-being by Sandra G. Turner, Carol P. Kaplan, and Lee W. Badger (2006/*Afflilia* 21(3): 272–281).

Body image and self-esteem among adolescent girls: Testing the influence of sociocultural factors by Daniel Clay, Vivian L. Vignoles, and Helga Dittmar (2005/*Journal of Research on Adolescence* 15(4): 451–477).

Body mass index, disordered eating behavior, and acquisition of health information: Examining ethnicity and weight-related issues in a college population by Shannon S. Rich and Christina R. Thomas (2008/*Journal of American College Health* 56(6): 623–628).

How investment in gender ideals affects well-being: The role of external contingencies of self-worth by Diana T. Sanchez and Jennifer Crocker (2005/*Psychology of Women Quarterly* 29: 63–77).

Integrating Black feminist thought into conceptual frameworks of African American adolescent women's sexual scripting processes by Dionne P. Stephens and Layli Phillips (2005/*Sexualities, Evolution and Gender* 7(1): 37–55).

Websites and Organizations

Aspira (www.aspira.org) is a national, nonprofit Hispanic organization committed to developing the intellectual and leadership skills of Hispanic youth within Puerto Rican and Latino communities.

Black Women for Black Girls (blackwomenforblackgirls.org) combines the knowledge base and financial resources of multiple programs focused on Black girls in New York City.

National Association of Anorexia Nervosa & Associated Disorders (www.anad.org) offers a listing of therapists, hospitals, and information materials, as well as advocacy campaigns, support group sponsorship, research, and a helpline (630-577-1330).

National Association for Media Literacy Education (namle.net) focuses on critical thinking, required in the media age, which empowers children and families to make informed decisions in any public or private space.

National Eating Disorders Association (www.nationaleatingdisorders.org) is a nonprofit organization focused on supporting individuals and families affected by eating disorders through prevention and treatment.

1. This U.S. policy, passed on February 1, 1996, and signed into law by President William Clinton on February 8, 1996, mandated that the television industry develop a ratings system to identify violent, sexual, and offensive or otherwise objectionable programming. The act also required the industry to manufacture sets with a V-chip ("V" for violence) that allowed parents to block objectionable subject matter.

2. Arnett, J. J. (1995). Adolescents' use of media for self-socialization. *Journal of Youth & Adolescence* 24: 519–533.

3. Bentley, M. K. (2002). The body of evidence: Dangerous intersections between development and culture in the lives of adolescent girls. In S. R. Mazzarella & N. O. Pecora (Eds.) *Growing up girls: Popular culture and the construction of identity* (209–221). New York: Peter Lang.

Chapter Three

Girls Will Be Boys

If I were a boy, even just for a day, I'd roll out of bed in the morning and throw on what I wanted and go. Drink beer with the guys and chase after girls. I'd kick it with who I wanted and I'd never get confronted for it 'cause they'd stick up for me. —"If I Were a Boy," —*Beyoncé*

Modesty used to be considered a natural female attribute. No more. —*Linda Chavez*

Even the most subjected person has moments of rage and resentment so intense that they respond, they act against. There is an inner uprising that leads to rebellion, however short-lived. It may be only momentary but it takes place. That space within oneself where resistance is possible remains. —*bell hooks*

U.S. schools have most recently been forced to confront the growing phenomenon of physically violent female students. According to the Department of Justice, schools around the country have been reporting an increase in the number of girls being suspended or expelled for using their fists to settle disputes. Although juvenile crime rates have been decreasing nationwide, the disparity between boys—who still commit an overwhelming majority of violent offenses—and girls has been lessening.

Data from the Office of Juvenile Justice and Delinquency Prevention observes that between 1995 and 2002 the rate of arrests for violent crimes among girls escalated, while the rates for boys decreased almost every year. Rising female violence has confused school and law enforcement officials as the assumption has always been that girls deal with their stress by withdrawing. We are seeing, however, just the opposite. Indeed, girls are threatening. They are outwardly violent. They are using knives, brass knuckles, and even guns.

In the Chicago Public School (CPS) system, violence has been increasing over the past several years. Violent episodes, whether in or on school grounds, climbed by almost 20 percent in 2009, with students committing aggravated battery, drug-related offenses, and assaults on school staff and personnel. Two societal factors are believed to be the primary causes of CPS's growing youth violence: *racial tension* and *gentrification*—both occurring mainly within Hispanic and Black communities with concentrated poverty.

The first factor is associated with Chicago's long history of segregation, which originated in the mid-1800s through racial prejudice and discriminatory business practices. Throughout the city's metropolitan area, class and racial lines of demarcation are drawn in nearly every direction, isolating ethnic groups by neighborhoods, blocks, and even streets. Chicago's economic patterns and cultural preferences maintain its status as a "dual-city"—one made up of principally White areas to the north, where vibrant economies persist and residents possess medium to high levels of income and formal educational backgrounds; the other city, to the south, east, and west, is primarily Black, Hispanic, and impoverished.

Whereas Chicago, and other U.S. cities, has a history of interracial conflict between Blacks and Whites, similar tensions are also known to exist between Black and Hispanic populations—two groups contending for various types of currency (e.g., political positions, school/community improvement plans, drug markets, and gang turf). Although hostilities exist between these racial groups, they also permeate within them as well. This is exemplified in instances where members of the same ethnicity are forced to reside in a shared community, leading to competition over limited resources. This convergence is one by-product of gentrification.

As part of the gentrification process, housing and business development initiatives transform the economic geographies of low-income areas into upper- or middle-income ones, forcing existing residents to move. This results in individuals being separated from long-established community heritage and values. Given the city's strikingly segregated demographics, displaced residents usually opt to move into neighborhoods of similar racial/ ethnic background. Even after settling into such areas, some relocated citizens wind up being mistreated or feeling unwanted by inhabitants already living there.

A parallel scenario also occurs within the CPS system. Schools reflecting the broader metropolis are thus disproportionately racially composed and segregated. When a campus closes, it requires its students to seek out another institution, often taking them far beyond their neighborhoods and across racial and gang territories. In schools where students of similar and/or different ethnicities have been plunged into the same academic environment, we have seen mounting levels of school violence that reflect community dynamics.[1]

In a city like Chicago, where travelling past one's block has deadly consequences, young people know all too well the risks they are taking just to get to school and back home. Community activists have linked the recent surge in youth violence to the city's educational initiative, Renaissance 2010.[2] At its inception, the average number of fatally shot CPS students, in 2005, was between ten and fifteen. In the 2006–2008 academic years, this figure rose to twenty-three deadly shootings. By 2009, there were a total of thirty-four public school student deaths by way of gun violence.

While larger socioeconomic factors can surely be correlated with the city's rising youth violence, this does not change the fact that it is an extremely urgent matter. Together with this issue, however, we must take a serious look at escalating levels of physically aggressive behaviors perpetrated by Black and Latina adolescent girls. Their conduct has lead to the perception that they are "worse than boys" when it comes to physical violence.

The issues that many Chicago public schools face, with respect to their female students, is not just about everyday classroom conflicts (e.g., fights over a boy or "he said, she said" scenarios), but also about gang rivalry in schools and communities. School social workers, counselors, and psychologists identify the most recent violent behaviors, exhibited by girls of color, as part of the *Code of the Street*, which justifies physical engagement as a viable solution to conflict.

Before discussing the cultural aspect of gender expectations and female aggression, we must first understand that the increasing participation of girls of color in violent acts is about more than just adaptation to surrounding community violence. For example, although seldom reported by news outlets, teenage girls, despite their racial and class backgrounds, are accounting for one out of four violent episodes in or outside of schools nationwide. The authors see this as directly connected to a present-day era of femininity that females across different cultural communities have been subscribing to.

While the old-fashioned feminine paradigm still exists, which ultimately delimits other facets of womanhood, girls and young women have been adopting multiple ways of thinking and being. This is witnessed not only in how girls demonstrate various models of femininity—via sports and male-centered academic disciplines such as math and science, but also in how they externalize typical male dispositions—being more outspoken, physically tougher, and aggressive toward peers. The observance of females becoming more "Alpha" has flipped conventional gender and sexual scripts upside-down, forcing our society to rethink antiquated ideals around "femaleness."

This "flipping" of scripts, as it were, is rooted, to some degree, in sociopolitical gains that have granted women entrée into traditionally male-dominated pursuits—vis-à-vis Title IX.[3] Women have since entered into various male-oriented arenas (e.g., academics, sports, politics), in spite of the perception that involvement in such fields was a contradiction to mainstream expectancies of womanhood and femininity. Girls, however, have not taken on male roles, and the behaviors associated with these roles, as a direct consequence of licensure. Rather, licensure has worked to transform America's male-centered terrain, creating multiple female images and ways of being that have given girls a range of ideas of what a woman can do and be.

This transposing of male and female scripts is notably less of a matter of *gender divergence* and more of *gender confluence*. Just as boys over the past few decades have been asked to become more attuned with their feminine side (i.e., being open, modest, tender), girls have also been pushed to become more in touch with their "inner male" (i.e., being tougher, more assertive, and ego-oriented).

As the larger gender landscape has apprised so many young women of their possibilities, smaller cultural spaces have also transmitted similar messages, some of which have been adopted from, and legitimatized by, mainstream society. U.S. slavery culturally redefined relationships between African-American women and men, as discussed in chapter 1, forcing Black women to be more authoritative and thus blurring the Eurocentric constructed gender line of the time.

Despite the historical context surrounding Black girls, we find within their cultural communities, as well as in Hispanic ones, that contemporary societal interpretations of femininity are also being added to their already existent cultural gender scripts. This augmenting has functioned to reinforce, for some, the already established cultural belief that they can do whatever boys can do, which includes excelling in virtually every aspect of academic and professional life. It, however, has also meant, given false and racialized representations of females of color, being labeled as overly sexual, aggressive, and violent by nature.

In view of our participants' expectations, as well as growing apprehension around girl violence, we asked them to give their perspective and offer some insight into this newly observed persona of girls "being like" boys. We begin the discussion with the phenomena of relational aggression and victimization and the ways in which girls and boys exert power over one another.

FROM WORDS TO FISTS, FROM GOSSIP TO GUNS

Toni

Toni is seventeen years old and African American. She describes herself as "funny, smart, and creative." She states that she has many life goals in mind—a photographer, an interior designer, a writer/poet, and a mother and wife—though she has neither a child nor a boyfriend at the present moment. Toni also says that she enjoys reading books and participating in her school's robotics club.

> I was bullied all the time. Like you get bullied if you're smart or if you're not popular. I was bullied emotionally and physically by different people in my school—girls and boys. You can tell the teachers and the principals, but they aren't going to do much about it. The boys always harass you because they want to have sex with you. So you pretty much get your butt slapped or get pushed up against the locker. Girls are more verbal. They'll call you "bitch" or "ho" or maybe not even talk to you. They're just emotionally abusive. They might say stuff like, "Oh, you slept with my ex-boyfriend," and all that stuff. That's how it always starts. Sometimes it's true, but not all the time. Everyone's different in their own little groups.

Toni's response speaks to her own experiences with relational aggression and sexual harassment that occurs primarily within the school setting. While we have introduced one mode of violence (physical) perpetrated by both girls and boys, relational aggression is another, yet is perceived as more characteristic of females. Although it includes a host of emotionally hurtful strategies used within female cliques, it can also be employed by boys. Girls, however, tend to be more highly skilled than boys at relational aggression as a result of the female expectation to mask feelings of anger.

At very early ages, girls learn to express emotion, resolve conflict, exert dominance, and achieve higher status through covert, interpersonal methods. Such methods consist of alienating peers from the larger group, gossiping about them, giving them the "silent treatment," stealing their friends or romantic interests, or isolating them altogether.

Among such tactics, which transpire within the physical world, is the fairly new phenomenon known as *cyberbullying*. Here, young people are able to take part in relationally aggressive acts, sometimes anonymously, by way of the electronic world—cell phones, online blogs and videos, as well as social networking websites. Even as the Internet represents an incredible informational tool, it also holds potential dangers for youth when its devices are manipulated to hurt others.

Concerning females of color, cultural scripts regarding femininity and emotional expression can run contrary to conventional techniques of relational aggression. One reason for this is embedded in the belief that familial socialization prepares these young women to confront oppression and discrimination in a more overt, proactive manner. Thus, in their attempt to separate themselves from disempowering historically based racial stigmas, African-American and Hispanic girls may use more assertive measures like speaking up and lashing out to avoid unfair treatment.

In spite of the sociocultural influences that prepare girls of color to be more forceful, we still find a majority of them turning to relational aggressive strategies. This is, in part, due to an acceptance of latent societal scripts that instruct them to mask emotions of anger, pain, and disappointment. The act of being "emotionally abusive" toward others, whether directly or indirectly, is a brand of violence that plays out in both schools and communities.

Even though relational aggression is considered, by and large, a function within gender, it can also encompass nuances of race, class, and ethnicity. For example, one peer group may employ relational aggressive practices against another individual or group, discriminating against them based on skin color, language, or social status. We witness this primarily within schools where youth are heavily concentrated.

Endemic of such discrimination and division is the proliferation of racial and class stereotypes, as well as institutional practices and policies that disregard student diversity. The psychological outcomes for students who are bullied through relational aggression are feelings of vulnerability, low self-esteem and self-worth, depression, and self-exclusion. The overall social consequence, particularly in the case of schools, is an atmosphere of ignorance, bigotry, and hatred.

Apposite to relational aggressive tactics initiated by females are the opprobrious acts of violence committed against them. These acts plague women worldwide and are inflicted upon them by virtue of their gender—physical assault, sexual harassment, and verbal and emotional abuse. As previously discussed, the patriarchal institution of *machismo* has been linked to physical control, sexual aggression, and power and force over women.

The "good" Latina is one who is virtuous and submissive to the male significant other. Chicanas and Latinas, firmly positioned within this male-female hierarchy, can experience relational victimization (i.e., extreme verbal and physical abuse) from their fathers, brothers, uncles, cousins, boyfriends, and husbands. Given their gender conditioning, these males often feel that it is their cultural right to be overprotective, if not sadistic, toward "their" women.

For African-American females, relational victimization also occurs within a hierarchy of gender oppression. The workings of male domination are so incredibly subtle and obscure that women within both cultures often feel a profound sense of self-blame and guilt when they are mistreated by their partner. The fact that Black girls and young women suffer domestic violence at higher rates than White females speaks to the normalized existence of the male authoritarian model in this cultural community—so normalized that Black males themselves are unaware of how they perpetuate and participate in the brutality and berating of women.

For both Black and Hispanic cultures, the male figure is one that wields respect and influence by reason of their position in a patriarchal society. Through methods of power and control, males in every society push women into self-defeating and powerless conditions that are damaging on all levels of their existence.

Relational victimization as experienced by women is not always committed by significant others. Female students certainly encounter such exploitative acts from peers, who have no considerable relational tie other than being a schoolmate—which in itself is a relation. Toni refers to this with regard to being verbally and physically accosted by her male peers: "The boys always harass you because they want to have sex with you. So you pretty much get your butt slapped or get pushed up against the locker."

This kind of gendered mistreatment is thought to extend from America's hypersexualized society that exposes small children to age-inappropriate images and conduct, which they may fail to synthesize due to their level of maturity and comprehension. As discussed in the previous chapter on media, children and adolescents can be indoctrinated into certain kinds of sexual behavior as it supplies them with information about gender scripts. In such cases, youth lack the ability to discern between what is harmful to someone else and the consequences of their own behavior. This is evidenced in high levels of sexual harassment that occur in schools daily.

In 2008, the American Civil Liberties Union (ACLU) reported that 81 percent of all elementary- and secondary-level students have experienced either unsolicited or unwanted sexual conduct during their school years. Though both girls and boys encounter sexual harassment at perplexing levels, girls experience it in larger proportion—85 percent of girls, as opposed to 76 percent of boys. The ACLU also found that girls who have been sexually harassed are more fearful while being in school and feel less positive about themselves than boys who have been harassed. These current statistics are interesting given that sexual harassment is illegal under Title IX legislation, which prohibits sex discrimination in federally funded schools.

A January 2010, front-page article from the *Chicago Tribune* entitled, "Sexually assaulted—and her school 'made it worse,'" features nineteen-year-old Gabrielle Smart, who as a sophomore, in 2006, claimed that she was sexually assaulted by her then-boyfriend and another classmate. The alleged attack took place during school hours in an apartment, just blocks away from their South Side school—Simeon Career Academy. Administrators, according to federal investigators, failed to protect Smart from incurring further threats from peers by permitting the suspected attackers to remain at the school weeks after the incident. Meghan Twohey, who covered the story, writes:

> Simeon is one of many high schools in Illinois to come under fire for their handling of student sexual assaults and dating-related violence. There are no state laws or policies governing how school districts should respond to these sensitive issues. . . .

When administrators fail to respond, students suffer humiliation, harassment and
other harm. . . . Some victims drop out. (1, 12)

Gabrielle, indeed, dropped out of Simeon in December 2006 and transferred
to another school district "to escape the fear and frustration" (12). Her ac-
cused assailants remained at Simeon up until the spring quarter, after which
they were finally expelled. In response to the Smart case, the Chicago Board
of Education strengthened its policy on sexual harassment among students
and employees.

Relational victimization, in the form of sexual harassment, occurring in or
outside of schools, is not about students expressing their affinity for one
another. It is not about flirting, nor is it about liking someone. It is more or
less about having control and influence over another individual or group.
This expressed power reveals itself in a variety of ways (i.e., through opposite-sex verbal insults and undesirable advances, as well as same-sex verbal
abuse and bodily harm).

In many instances, because young people are unconscious of the sexual
scripts that they have been exposed to, they are also unaware of what consti-
tutes sexual harassment, much less relational victimization. Nevertheless, as
adults working with children and adolescents, we cannot ignore such behaviors and chalk it up to boys being boys or girls being girls. When Toni
declares that "you can tell the teachers and the principals, but they aren't
going to do much about it," we have essentially propagated a climate of
violence and a culture of silence, where young people can incur serious
injuries to their mind, body, and spirit.

Lapita

A girl doesn't need to be sitting down all quietly. I mean, somebody's gonna end up
getting on your nerves and you're gonna get mad. You're going to eventually do
something, say something, fight or whatever. That doesn't have to mean you're a
boy. If you cuss, that doesn't mean you're a boy. You can be nice and stuff. You
know a girl that's nice can be very nice, but if you get mad, you just get mad. You
might have that boy, the so-called boy, the not-so-good boy inside of you and you let
it out. You let your anger out. If somebody comes to me and says we gonna fight,
then we gonna fight because I'm not the type of person to back down. I'm not just
gonna sit there and get treated. I'm gonna get mad and I'm gonna get up and be like
if you want to fight, let's fight. I mean boys can fight. Why can't girls fight? They
say fighting might not solve things, but sometimes it does. You might have to
whoop somebody just to get them away from you and leave you alone. You have to
show that you're not afraid or scared.

Lapita's comment above is riddled with dichotomous notions around culturally defined feminine roles versus normative ones. In one breath, she states
that a girl "that's nice can be very nice," yet there are moments when "if you

get mad, you just get mad. . . . You let your anger out." Her perceptive remark speaks to two opposing ideals of femaleness—the rough, tomboy girl and the emotional, introverted one.

What is significant to note here is that, even as these constructions on the surface are disparate, they ostensibly exist within Lapita as a single identity. She affirms this: "A girl doesn't need to be sitting down all quietly. . . . If you cuss, that doesn't mean you're a boy. You can be nice and stuff." This is an indication that she has not utterly abandoned her feminine side and wholly taken on masculine traits. Quite the opposite. Lapita refers to this aspect of her identity as "the not-so-good boy inside" that some girls let out. External perceptions of these two opposite female constructions might sexually misconstrue and label the tomboy girl as masculine or homosexual.

Conversely, the emotional girl might be regarded as feminine and thus "normative." Through the lens of social class and race, the rough and "ready to fight" girl might be stigmatized as "ghetto" or uncouth, whereas the introverted girl might be perceived as more urbane or refined—two polarizing representations that are as stark as day and night, yet could also be perceived as shades of grey.

Lapita goes on to add, "I mean boys can fight. Why can't girls fight?" Though a straightforward question, it holds vast perplexities. The authors address Lapita's query in two fundamental ways: (1) from a social perspective and (2) from an individual one. When society conflates fighting girls with masculine behavior, it fails to see this type of female conduct as a dimension of femininity or femaleness. That is, given the manner in which female behavior is defined in our patriarchal society, physically aggressive girls will then be perceived as having abandoned their womanhood in order to adopt masculine traits, consequently leaving them to be judged in the same way as males.

From *Girls' Violence: Beyond Dangerous Masculinity*,[4] Irwin and Chesney-Lind (2008) write:

> At its core, masculinization is a gender similarities perspective because it assumes that the same forces that propel men into violence will increasingly produce violence in girls and women once they are freed from the constraints of their gender. In fact, masculine theories of female violence reinforce the historic problem with universal theories of crime. They imply that contemporary theories of violence (and crime, more broadly) need not attend to gender, but can simply "add women and stir." Since girls and women are now acting more like boys and men and gaining access to traditionally male settings, the theories will work to explain girls' behavior. (839–840)

Although girls' motivations for fighting may be comparable to that of boys, we must be careful in strictly looking at females through a masculine lens. The idea of "add women and stir" situates girls within masculine frames of behavior that faultily compare their motivation for violence to that of boys. This has resulted in biased judgments and penalties against females in schools and in juvenile justice systems.[5]

Overlooking the rationale as to why girls and young women employ violence, and thus assessing them within masculine contexts, can be regarded as yet another form of violence that silences their feminine voice, identity, and possible circumstances around victimization. In doing so, we also narrow the scope of female multidimensionality, categorizing or "other"-izing girls and women, without acknowledging the deep impact that patriarchal systems, relationships, and theories have on their personal lives.

From an individual standpoint, the question of: "Why can't girls fight?" speaks to more than just females wholly embracing male traits. When Lapita refers to the "not-so-good boy inside," she is, essentially, alluding to the typical male reaction to rage, which emerges from within Lapita: "I'm not the type of person to back down. I'm not just gonna sit there and get treated. I'm gonna get mad and I'm gonna get up and be like if you want to fight, let's fight."

Lapita's comment is linked to the long-established sexualized script that says males are able to express anger in an outwardly physical manner, which for females is regarded as unfeminine or atypical. Yet, once again, the "boy inside" is only one facet of her identity. This characteristic of Lapita does not make her any less feminine, but it does give us a greater sense of the ambiguous nature of gender, as well as the set cultural and social expectations that we apply to it. To further unpack the issue of female violence—personal and sociocultural—let us briefly attend to why some females of color feel the need to turn to physical aggression in the first place.

With respect to girls and young women overall, physical violence can be employed as a manner of challenging pervasive societal messages that violence is immoral, unfeminine, and relationally caustic. Girls may resort to violence as a means of communicating anger against past or present victimizations, expressing a level of resilience, defending themselves, or displaying authority and control over others. Irwin and Chesney-Lind (2008) claim:

> Girls' aggression can send a strong "don't mess with me" signal to others. Violence, therefore, can be reactionary and proactive, instrumental and expressive, protective and retaliatory, rational and irrational. Girls' violence can result from pro-violence rationalizations, motives, and rewards received from friends, boyfriends, or family members. It can signal all the ways that girls are "down for" their friends or their gang. (848)

A great deal of sociological research proposes that Black and Hispanic youth use violence as an instrument to achieve dominant femininities and masculinities within spaces where they perceive being disenfranchised by White, middle-class power relations and structures that are supposed to address their needs (e.g., schools). While the explanations that Irwin and Chesney-Lind provide are applicable to all girls and young women, females of color living in fragmented communities can be affected, like boys, by unique neighborhood conditions that require a tough exterior and a swift ability to be combative.

Whether a young woman is well-adjusted or not, she may still have to resort to violence in order to deal with such encounters as school or neighborhood fights; aggressive arguments with peers; their boyfriends, or their baby's father; sexual assaults; burglaries; or drive-bys. In some cases, girls of color are explicitly told by parents to fight their own battles through words or fists.

It becomes exceptionally difficult for nonfamilial adults (e.g., teachers, principals, mentors) to advise young people against physical violence as a solution to problems, when they are receiving dissimilar instructions within the home. It is also unlikely that youth will be able to rise above violent confrontations and turn the other cheek, when all around them is the expectation and demand to be tough and reactionary.

Female violence is an enormously complex phenomenon because we are talking about newer and more evident ways in which girls and young women are expressing their rage. As such, there are no easy answers for addressing how we should deal with this issue. While girls rely on violent behavior for the same reasons as boys, differences do emerge in matters of victimization between the sexes. For instance, there is a vast distinction between girls brawling due to a dispute that sparked physical confrontation versus a girl defending herself in response to being pushed up against a locker and fondled.

Within these two scenarios, separate analyses should be thoroughly considered in how violence was provoked, as well as its outcome. The task of teachers, principals, and disciplinarians is to be cognizant of and sensitive to those personal situations that dictate the use of violence within and between the sexes and the judgments that are passed down. Without doing so, we become complicit in placing girls into constricted, male-oriented theories of violence that simply claim, "Add women and stir."

Angelica

Angelica is nineteen and Mexican-American. She perceives herself as "smart and nice." In her interview, she openly admitted to formerly being involved in a gang. She states, "I used to gang bang mainly because I didn't have no love. I didn't have a mom or dad. My grandma used to beat me anyway, so I thought I might as well join something that had lesser beatings, more love, and more money to help me get a place to live." Angelica has left gang life far behind her since having a baby and getting married. After graduation from high school, she intends to become a certified nursing assistant.

> Some girls be friends one day and then next thing you know they go behind your back calling you names and saying you slept with this guy or talking about your boyfriend. But girls will fight each other too. Like some Latinas, we don't scratch. We bring out blades, bats, and golf clubs. And we mostly fighting about the same thing like boyfriends and ex-men, or a baby's daddy or sometimes it can be gang related. Like, sometimes when girls pick up their baby from daycare, they start the drama in front of their kids and start fighting and shooting. I remember one time I seen a girl walking down the street and because these other girls didn't like her, they shot her baby. And that's just girls shooting girls. You also see girls shooting boys, boys shooting girls, and boys shooting boys. There's no difference. It's the same thing.

Angelica's commentary above conveys the more intensely hostile reactionary and retaliatory side of female violence, further blurring the constructs of femininity and masculinity. Interesting to underscore here is the participant's sense that there is no reason "why girls can't fight." Indeed they can. They not only can fight, they can also shoot. For her, there is "no difference" between males and females with respect to the aggression that they perpetrate ("We bring out blades, bats, and golf clubs"). While Angelica observes that females may resort to violence to handle conflict with males, she also states that gang affiliation plays a role.

Street gangs are widely considered a by-product of social disorganization and failing institutions, such as schools and welfare programs. Though typically thought of as an urban phenomenon, we are recognizing that gangs also exist and remain active in suburban and rural settings, as well as in domestic and international military installations. According to some experts, a vast majority of gang members are youth under the age of eighteen who live in disjointed inner-city communities.

Street gangs tend to comprise members from the same racial or ethnic background. The reasons for their establishment can range anywhere from protecting community residents from outsider violence to defending neighborhood "turf" and from drug trade and trafficking to affording youth with a sense of family and belongingness. Despite the kinships that are developed within gangs, they still represent one of the most destructive forces to communities. While cities like Chicago face the challenge of school violence, a more prevalent threat to school-aged youth is the deadly bloodshed initiated by gang warfare.

In 2009, the National Gang Intelligence Center reported that street gangs in the Unites States climbed to an estimated one million members, responsible for 80 percent of crimes in local communities. The center's current projection has 900,000 gang members residing within urban sectors across the country, with 147,000 in U.S. jails or prisons.

Data on the number of female youth gang members has been particularly hard to gather, since their affiliations often function in one of three major categories: *autonomous all-female units, mixed-sex gangs,* and *auxiliaries.* All-female units are the rarest of these categories, with mixed-sex and auxiliaries being more common. Although gangs are still by and large a male-dominated enterprise, figures on female membership (somewhere between 60,000 and 80,000) disclose that girl gangs are on the rise in cities like Chicago, New York, Washington, Boston, and Los Angeles.

In the past, female gangs have not been on America's radar. Traditionally, we have responded to girls' delinquent conduct by relying upon intervention programs to sort out their maladjustment. However, now that we are seeing girls and young women become more involved with criminal activities, these young people are beginning to garner more of our attention.

Some of the things that we know about female gang members are this:

- The ethnic background of most members is either African-American or Latina.
- About 40 percent of membership is teenagers.
- They come from dysfunctional, abusive, and/or low-income families.
- They have had little to no involvement in positive school programs or activities.
- They experience early drug use and sexual activity.
- They carry and use knives, bats, brass knuckles, and guns.
- They commit fewer crimes and minor violent offenses, as compared to males (e.g., simple battery and assault, drug use, petty theft or robbery, and domestic violence such as fights with parents or boy/girlfriends).
- An overwhelming majority of adolescent girls in correctional facilities are gang affiliated—of this population, 26 percent have been in special education, 65 percent suffer from psychological issues, and 70 percent have been victimized or sexually abused as a child.

When we talk about fighting girls, we are essentially talking about females who use violence as a conveyance of power. Gangs, in part, represent that conduit that imbues them with a sense of desired control and exuded force that becomes indispensable as they are living in spaces where they can be powerless (i.e., the perceived incapacity to transform their lives and the world around them). Gangs can offer females voice, purpose, recognition, and a space to bond with others who are experiencing related life issues such as abuse, abandonment, and a need for independence.

Just as Angelica claims: "I didn't have no love. I didn't have a mom or dad. My grandma used to beat me anyway, so I thought I might as well join something that had lesser beatings, more love, and more money to help me get a place to live." The type of solidarity that gangs provide can be extremely important for females, and young people generally, who are striving to form a sense of identity, develop their autonomy, become financially stable, and determine what their talents and abilities might be within community spaces of limited choice and access.

For females of color, gangs can further provide an escape from normalizing cultural standards of gender and femininity that marginalize their oppositional self. As *machismo* stresses that women be pure, nurturing, and compliant, some Latinas attempt to detach themselves from this construct vis-à-vis gang life. This entails accepting codes and engaging in high-risk activities that reflect the traditional male world—dressing masculine, carrying guns, and being sexually promiscuous.

The irony is that, despite the parity and respect that they seek, females' position within gangs can reflect larger societal ideals around gender roles. For instance, within auxiliaries, girls and young women take on minor, assistant-type responsibilities such as serving as a lookout, transporting small amounts of drugs, and carrying guns for male members.

Female gang participation is also viewed as more gender divergent rather than confluent. As such, female gang members, whether African-American, Chicana, or Puerto Rican, face being labeled a "tomboy," "thug," or "lesbian." The students we spoke with contested many of these stigmas as they still see themselves as feminine, and believe that their male significant others view them the same way, regardless of their "boy-like" conduct.

In *Chicana Adolescents: Bitches, 'Ho's, and Schoolgirls,*[6] Lisa Dietrich unpacks some of the complexities around female gang membership and the tension girls encounter in their quest for gender equity:

> One way that the homegirls manage conflict between their gender and their gang affiliation is by adopting masculine clothing styles and mannerisms. Gang-affiliated girls can be distinguished from their nongang female counterparts in terms of their dress, language, and mannerisms/behavior. . . . However, in spite of the overt masculinity associated with gang membership, the homegirls do not reject all feminine behaviors. They spend great amounts of money and time on their makeup, hair, and jewelry. Girl gang members perceive themselves as liberated from many of the constraints of traditional feminine behavior, yet they still want to be accepted by the homeboys as essentially feminine, sexually attractive girls. The homegirls walk a fine line between their desire for parity with the male gang members and their desire to be sexually attractive to them. (152)

The authors asked Angelica about the dress and mannerisms of girl gang members and how their external appearance raises questions about their sexual orientation. From her gang experience, Angelica informed us that, while some girls may very well be bisexual or lesbian, she believed that a majority of them are heterosexual. She also added that girls' participation in street gangs is more about status and protection as opposed to a preoccupation with homosexuality.

Even though societal perceptions of female gang members position girls beyond the lines of the traditional gender box, their affiliation is not entirely about gender divergence. We contend that their involvement represents just one of the ways in which females reject oppressive forces that are rooted in economics and patriarchy. The fact that they still confront gender tensions, within gangs associated with femininity, speaks to the stifling power of gender norms and expectations.

Gang involvement, in its simplest and most intricate framework, functions, for some females, as an organizing tool in resistance to victimization. That said, the authors are by no means justifying or romanticizing the role of street gangs. There is no question that they hurt their communities and themselves. Our goal here was to simply provide additional contexts by which to explain girl violence and why gangs have particular meaning for adolescent females of color.

CLOSING COMMENT AND RECOMMENDED RESOURCES

Violence is an American ritual. It is rooted in our history, torrent in our media, and omnipresent in our daily lives. We are addicted to it, captivated by it. We freely allow it to consume us. Violence conveyed through guns, knives, or fists, however, are manifestations of how severe socioeconomic dynamics produce hostile human responses. These dynamics are the ways in which we marginalize, prohibit, and disempower individuals from taking advantage of their basic human right to equity and access.

The "culture of poverty" tells us that poor Whites, Blacks, and Hispanics are autonomous in their decision making and that their failure to achieve socioeconomic success is a result of their own "defects." You combine this perspective with the American slogan "equality of opportunity," and it is quite easy to dismiss the greater burning issue of "equality of condition." The latter speaks to the "culture of segregation," where structural conditions produce and perpetuate inequity as it divides the poor from the middle class, continuously limiting their opportunities to engage in the larger economy.

Residential segregation inflates concentrated poverty, as well as other forms of racial oppression. This is a key factor to consider in the equation of community violence. For females and males of color who reside in neighborhoods that struggle with such conditions as rising unemployment, failing institutions, neglected housing, and high crime, reactions to oppressive climates often call for an exceptionally tough outer shell. For this reason alone, we must understand that aggressive responses from adolescent girls of color, while in part a cultural expectation, are intensified when fused with high-stress stimuli found within impoverished communities.

One method to address youth violence is to speak with young people, listen to their voices, understand the reasons behind their conduct, and help them in interpreting their choices and actions. Another way (and perhaps the most complex of strategies) is to dismantle areas of concentrated poverty altogether. While poor and low-income families are no less dedicated than middle-class families to caring and providing for themselves, the socioeconomic inequities that they face will subsist without true structural change in the expansion of residential options.

Books

8 Ball Chicks by Gini Sikes (1997/Anchor Books).
Black Sexual Politics: African Americans, Gender, and the New Racism by Patricia Hill-Collins (2005/Routledge).
Code of the Street: Decency, Violence, and the Moral Life of the Inner City by Elijah Anderson (2000 /W. W. Norton & Company).
Making the Second Ghetto: Race and Housing in Chicago 1940–1960 by Arnold R. Hirsch (1998/University of Chicago Press).
Mexican American Girls and Gang Violence: Beyond Risk by Avelardo Valdez (2009/Palgrave Macmillan).
Odd Girl Out: The Hidden Culture of Aggression in Girls by Rachel Simmons (2002/Harcourt Books).
Social Justice and the City by David Harvey (2009/University of Georgia Press).
Why We Hate Black Women: Deconstructing the Paradox of Black Female Masculinity by Hasani Pettiford (2010/Blue Magic Publishing).

Articles

Adjudicated adolescent girls and their mothers: Examining identity perceptions and processes by Jennifer L. Kerpelman and Sondra L. Smith (1999/*Youth and Society* 30: 313–347).
Adolescent girls' alcohol use as a risk factor for relationship violence by Wendy Marsh Buzy, Renee McDonald, Ernest N. Jouriles, Paul R. Swank, David Rosenfield, Jennifer S. Shimek, and Deborah Corbitt-Shindler (2004/*Journal of Research on Adolescence* 14(4): 449–470).
Developmental trajectories of bullying and associated behaviors by Debra Pepler, Depeng Jiang, Wendy Craig, and Jennifer Connolly (2008/*Child Development* 79(2): 325–338).
Girl power in a digital world: Considering the complexity of gender, literacy, and technology by Bronwyn T. Williams (2007/*Journal of Adolescent and Adult Literacy* 50(4): 300–307).
In protection of ourselves: Black girls' perceptions of self-reported delinquent behaviors by Aalece O. Pugh-Lilly, Helen A. Neville, and Karen L. Poulin (2001/*Psychology of Women Quarterly* 25: 145–154).
Navigating power, control, and being nice: Aggression in adolescent girls' friendships by Laura M. Crothers, Julaine E. Field, and Jered B. Kolbert (2005/*Journal of Counseling and Development* 83: 349–354).
Peer regulation of teenage sexual identities by Deborah Chambers, Estella Tincknell, and Joost Van Loon (2004/*Gender and Education* 16(3): 397–415).
Psychosocial correlates of dating violence victimization among Latino youth by Donna E. Howard, Kenneth Beck, Melissa Hallmark Kerr, and Teresa Shattuck (2005/*Adolescence* 40(158): 319–331).

Websites and Organizations

Boys and Girls Club of America (www.bgca.org) has presently expanded its services to include antiviolence and gang prevention programs.

The National Alliance of Gang Investigators' Associations (www.nagia.org) is a cooperative organization with a partnership of seventeen regional gang investigator associations and over 15,000 gang investigators across the country, as well as federal agencies and other organizations involved in gang-related issues.

The National Association of Students Against Violence Everywhere (www.nationalsave.org) is a nonprofit that is for and led by young people at elementary, middle, secondary, and college levels of education. The association currently networks with schools and other organizations in forty-six states and several foreign countries.

StreetGangs.com (www.streegangs.com) is a website that offers a comprehensive list of active intervention, prevention, and antiviolence programs in the Los Angeles area.

1. In 2007, Austin High School—a majority African-African campus—was shut down, sending most of its students to Roberto Clemente Community Academy—a majority Hispanic campus. One of the critical outcomes of this merging was daily scuffles that occurred between neighborhood Clemente students and those newly arriving from Austin. Some of the violence breaking out in Clemente was gang-related.

2. Renaissance 2010 is an ongoing initiative, originally launched in 2005 by Chicago Mayor Richard Daley and then CPS Chief Executive Officer Arne Duncan. Its primary goal has been to replace academically failing and low-enrollment schools with one hundred new "high-quality" schools in the form of charters and small campuses across Chicago by 2010. Since 2005, dozens of CPS schools have been closed, reassigning thousands of primary- and secondary-level students to other school locations within the city.

3. Title IX of the Educational Amendments of 1972, later renamed after its principal author in 2002, the Patsy T. Mink Opportunity in Education Act, is the landmark legislation that banned sex discrimination in schools in academics and athletics. Prior to Title IX, many schools refused to allow access to women or enforced rigid limits upon them. Since its enactment, women have made tremendous gains in the areas of sports as well as education—medical, law, and doctoral degrees.

4. Irwin, K., & Chesney-Lind, M. (2008). Girls' Violence: Beyond Dangerous Masculinity. *So ciology Compass* 2/3: 837–855.

5. As suspension and expulsion rates climb among girls of color, so too has their representation, as adult women, in the criminal justice system. The American Civil Liberties Union reported, in 2007, that African-American women made up 13 percent of the U.S. female population and Hispanic women 11 percent. Latinas represented 16 percent of all incarcerated women in the U.S., with Black women at 30 percent. Within the court system, low-income females of color experience discriminatory punishments with more intensity, often receiving the same harsh punishments (i.e., jail or prison terms) as males. For example, drug offenses can carry the same charge, regardless of the woman's role in the crime—whether acting as the primary offender or pressured into the act by a boyfriend or husband.

6. Dietrich, L. C. (1998). *Chicana Adolescents: Bitches, 'Ho's, and Schoolgirls*. Westport, Connecticut: Praeger.

Chapter Four

A Family Affair

It is easy to love the people far away. It is not always easy to love those close to us. It is easier to give a cup of rice to relieve hunger than to relieve the loneliness and pain of someone unloved in our own home. Bring love into your home for this is where our love for each other must start. —*Mother Teresa*

Everyone needs a strong sense of self. It is our base of operations for everything that we do in life. —*Julia Alvarez*

Family support plays an essential role in the positive growth and development of young people worldwide. Whether they are traditionally nuclear, single-parent, extended, or nonbiological, the family ideally represents a tremendous source of love, safety, comfort, and guidance for youth. Throughout childhood and adolescence, family support is especially crucial in instances where young people feel alienated or neglected by the surrounding world. Vast amounts of research all point to the fact that families are an indispensable resource in helping youth foster resiliency and filling potential voids of angst, dejection, and depression.

Although families offer a level of intimacy and nurturance for youngsters, they can also render a fair amount of anxiety and conflict. These tensions exist in various forms and degrees—divorce, remarriage, sibling rivalries, verbal or physical abuse, changes in employment or financial status, academic pressuring, or the passing of a family member.

In the adolescent years, family tensions can surface when teens begin retreating from childhood parental attachments, pushing for greater independence and personal responsibility. When teens begin ignoring parental authority, the resulting perception is that they are no longer in need of family support or security. Family members, especially parents, can interpret adolescents' shifting attitudes and dyadic relationships in a negative light and actively work to control youth through discipline—at times, fueling more opposition and frustration for all involved.

For teenagers, sweeping hormonal changes, as well as an expanding conceptual mind, finds them in rather vexed positions regarding their identity, friendships, sexual behavior, expectations, and social roles. This can engender feelings of confusion and the belief that no one understands them, including their parents. While adolescents, on the surface, may appear to be the "rebel without a cause," most of them actually have a goal in mind—that is, answering the mostly unconscious question, "Who is the true me?" In addressing this query, teenagers often strain ties with parents and family members. The intent is not necessarily to have complete separation from their family, but rather to create just enough space and time to figure out who they are in the present moment.

Whereas the family served to shape the childhood personality, adolescence marks the period when youngsters require additional insights about the world, and thus seek out nonfamilial sources for this information. Understanding the trials and errors that teens will face during this quest situates the role of families, and the support they can provide, as even more pivotal in this stage of development.

Urban communities, as opposed to suburban or rural ones, are typically characterized, and even stigmatized, as areas of dense poverty and violence. All of the adolescent women featured in this book reside in various working-class communities of Chicago. We have chosen to examine the intricate nature of families and parenting within this specific context as it poses a range of diverse opportunities, experiences, and problems for those youth living in the inner city.

Although urban settings comprise a range of socioeconomic classes, the harsh reality is that just over 40 percent of the nation's poor live in urban sectors that endure insufficient housing, underemployment, pollution, high levels of crime, and substandard schools. In fact, many U.S. cities find that at least a third of their citizens are unable to adequately have basic needs met with regard to shelter, water, health care, sanitation, and education. Women are disproportionately impacted by this as they tend to be the poorest with the added responsibility of children.

Sociologists and educational scholars alike argue that concentrated poverty, within urban areas, is an intensely racialized phenomenon. Though poor Whites make up almost twice the number of metropolitan residents, compared to poor African-Americans and Hispanics, they are more likely dispersed and living in mixed-income areas with working- and middle-class families, who have access to broader resources.

A larger percentage of poor Black and Latino families, on the other hand, are clustered in racially segregated working-class and poor neighborhoods. The grave outcome for some of these families is that they have fewer resources and limited access to adequate social services and systems to support a better quality of life. In areas of extreme poverty, institutions like schools and hospitals are severely underfunded to the point of erosion. This creates further difficulties for families beyond their own personal financial struggles.

Sociologist Rand Conger's *Family Stress Model* (1988) suggests that poverty places enormous amounts of pressure onto families, leading to emotional distress and dysfunction. Conger and his colleagues gathered data from nearly 1,500 families, from African-American and Euro-American backgrounds, who were residing in urban and rural areas. Their findings showed that poverty, or a major loss of income, escalated feelings of sadness, depression, and cynicism about the future among family members. According to Conger, when hostility and hopelessness pervades home life, parents can become less effective and children become more detached, feeling less support, consistency, and love.

Although the adversities facing urban youth and families of color can be compared across other racial groups, residing in or outside of the inner city, research insists that minority groups from the most disadvantaged communities drastically encounter higher levels of stress, negative social effects, and greater limitations in healthily managing their conditions. In disjointed urban spaces, families have to cope with the day-to-day struggles of gang violence, failing schools with zero-tolerance policies, community policing, insufficient health care, and dilapidated housing. When family structures are disrupted by the above factors, children and adolescents may often feel the direct impact.

A family's reaction, and internalized behavior, to harsh urban conditions is partially determined by the strength of the members within it. Even though some research would lead us to believe that the general response to poverty is violence, that result is not always the case. Poverty and low-income status definitely poses serious life challenges to the family unit. However, there are those families who strive daily to keep their organization intact and to support their youngest members.

Resiliency models identify six general characteristics[1] that help families surmount the complex interplay between privation and dysfunction:

1. *Adaptability*—being able to cope with different types of stress.
2. *Communication*—genuinely listening and respecting the opinions and beliefs of others.
3. *Community resources*—being involved and connected to community members and organizations (e.g., extended family, schools, churches, health-care facilities).
4. *Dedication*—being committed to the family system and acknowledging the worth of every member.
5. *Encouragement*—supporting the positive efforts of one another.

6. *Ethics*—strong family values and appropriate behavior are instilled in each family member.

Regardless of their socioeconomic status, Black and Hispanic families possess and utilize social capital resources such as extended family members, neighbors, churches, schools, and community businesses. For disadvantaged families, these relationships are intensely more vital as they help moderate some of the ill effects of poverty and institutional racism through financial assistance, spiritual guidance, and emotional support.

As for our participants, we found that beyond their own intrinsic strengths, they receive a level of encouragement from significant others in handling adversity. We asked some of them to discuss the significance of this support and what it means in their respective lives.

BLOOD IS THICKER THAN MUD

Mira

My family plays a big role in my life. They always supported me even though I got pregnant. I wasn't even out of high school. I was young. They didn't throw me out on the streets or nothing. My mom does a lot stuff for me. Like she'll watch the baby because she knows I gotta go to school.

Nikki

My family's real important. They keep me grounded; they stay on me; they tell me the truth when I need to hear it and when I don't want to hear it. Like my foster mother, she's true blue to the end. She's another one of the people who really got me to come back to school. I dropped out my sophomore year, and she knew that I had a purpose and that I could make it. I couldn't see it right then and there, but I see it now.

Simone

Simone is eighteen years old. She is first-generation Belizean-American with a faint Caribbean accent. She describes herself as, "joyful, understanding, and hardworking." After graduating from high school, Simone plans to attend college and make a good living. In addition to being on the honor roll, she spends weekends volunteering for various nonprofit community organizations.

Family's there for you. Even if you do wrong, they try to make you feel better. They don't make you feel bad about everything you do. They may say that was bad, but next time you'll do better. You know, and that'll help you even in school. If you got a D or an F on your test, family supports you and tells you to study more. They try to be more involved and tell you that it'll be better.

The parallel theme woven throughout all three student responses is the weight family support has in relation to their academic careers. These girls have struggled, and continue to struggle, with schooling. Yet the assistance they receive from their respective parents and guardians functions to keep them on track and inspired. Whether it is their mother, foster mother, or relatives, it appears that these young women remain resilient with the aid of their families.

Definitions of resilience are comparable across the research. As there is no clear-cut definition of the term, resilience usually refers to the capacity to bounce back successfully and to develop social competence in the face of severe stress. Literature on adolescent resilience leans more toward social and psychological forces that help individuals rise above difficult situations that would otherwise add to dysfunction.

The ability to overcome hardship with the assistance of protective factors is based on *Resiliency Theory*. The notion proposes that if members of one's family, community, and/or school express genuine care, hold high expectations, and are supportive, then the individual will have enough confidence in the future to overcome virtually any hardship.

Studies on resiliency among African-American and Latino youth are growing within the research literature. However, while there is still an abundance of work that focuses on why youth of color either fail or succeed academically, there is less conversation about which protective factors foster resiliency among these young people.

Existent research on resilience in Black and Hispanic youth often point to family and extended family members as key factors in providing young people with strong feelings of self-worth and emotional security, as well as a sense of control over personal successes and failures. Resilience, for this group, is also thought to be fostered by nonfamilial/nonparental community members such as teachers, coaches, mentors, and church leaders. In this context, external resources made available to the family can help determine the advancement of the child.

As evidenced in the comments above, all three participants view family support as instrumental in keeping them focused on education, despite facing various stressors. Mira's mother shows her support by looking after Mira's child in order for her to attend school; Nikki's foster care mom exhibits her encouragement by keeping Nikki "grounded"; Simone's family shows support by continually uplifting her, even when she fails to make high marks. These familial relationships are consistent with current resiliency research, which posits that students of color with a strong sense of self-worth and direction come from homes where there is positive interaction, effective communication, and strong family values.

Although the young women above are accorded a relative measure of family support around their academic attainment, not all of the young women in this book receive it. In the next section, we examine parent support and involvement in schools as it has become a critical issue in the field of education. Later, in chapter 5, we will look more closely at the schooling experiences of our participants with respect to student-teacher relationships.

Research suggests that parental involvement holds a level of promise for improving the overall learning environment for school participants—better student grades and attendance, fewer dropouts, increased positive attitudes regarding school and homework, enhanced job satisfaction among teachers, and greater student and parent satisfaction with their school. However, there has been recent finger-pointing by educators and politicians in the direction of parents from primarily working-class, inner-city areas, for their supposed lack of interest in their child's education.

Black and Hispanic working-class parents' failure to participate in school affairs (e.g., report card pick-up, parent-teacher conferences, and homework assistance) is often interpreted as an unabashed disregard for education. These parents are repeatedly stereotyped as "apathetic," "difficult to reach," or "not educated enough" to assist their child with schoolwork. It is quite easy to imagine how such labels can strain associations between families and schools and produce distrust between the two parties.

While there are parents who willfully abdicate their role in assisting their child with school, these parents do not reflect the vast majority. Remember: *Intracultural and individual variances in attitudes and behaviors within cultural groups must be considered.* In order to move beyond oversimplification, we must recognize some of the complex economic, structural, and cultural barriers that minimize the involvement of urban parents. Doing so allows school practitioners to view families more clearly, developing stronger, more engaging relationships through empathy, trust, and awareness.

One barrier facing parents of color is workload. Many children attending public city schools are from low-income, single-parent households, where the mom is usually the sole provider. Studies over the past several years have found that single or unmarried mothers experience more stresses than their married counterparts, with respect to financial burdens such as income for basic needs. In order to make ends meet, single parents can work long hours at one or more jobs that require multiple responsibilities. In some cases, their work schedule not only restricts the time they have for being at schools, but also their time for assisting their children with homework.

What is more, challenging work schedules may render single parents practically absent in the household. When they are not always around to reassure their children that they are safe at home, schools turn out to be more secure environments where youngsters can obtain the attention they need from peers, teachers, and other adults. Some single parents may feel a level of guilt for not being available or involved in school affairs that have significance for their children. Yet their hands are often tied with the choices they have, given their financial stresses and time constraints.

Language is another barrier that can negatively impact parent involvement. In this current age of school reform, specialized vocabulary, also known as *edspeak*, is expanding by the minute. It envelops educators and becomes a part of their everyday written and oral communications. For parents, edspeak can be fairly difficult to understand. When the use of such *educationese* terms as "authentic assessment,"[2] "detracking"[3] and "standards-based education"[4] becomes a routine or unconscious way of speaking to parents, the result may not only be their confusion, but also their belittlement.

"Edspeak" is representative of a particular occupation, where its usage is foreign to those who are external to the profession. Once language goes over one's head, it can distance an individual, if not intimidate them. As parents may already be stressing over personal life issues, fearing that they will be bombarded with a lexicon of educational jargon to describe their child's academic standing is not the most successful way to garner their involvement.

For Hispanic parents, specifically those with limited English proficiency, language is recognized as a huge barrier to school participation. Some Hispanic parents feel that because of the language divide, they are powerless to make a difference in their children's education. Others maintain that in spite of their limited English, low levels of education, and sparse economic resources, they are still able to provide learning opportunities for their children.

Unfortunately, educators largely associate students' low-income and non-English-speaking skills with student failure. Returning back to some of the stereotypes that typify noninvolved parents, Latinos from poor communities or of recent immigration are frequently blamed for not participating in schools as a direct result of their socioeconomic and cultural status. This type of finger-pointing produces an uninviting school atmosphere, leading parents to be noninvolved, where they otherwise might have been.

Regarding teacher perceptions of non-English-speaking Hispanic parents, from *Involving Latino Families in Schools: Raising Achievement through Home-School Partnerships*,[5] Concha Delgado Gaitan writes:

> Ultimately, this is translated as the parents not valuing education and not caring about their children's schooling. Parents, in turn, claim that they don't have enough time, they don't feel welcome in school, they don't speak English, they don't understand the school system, they don't have child care, and they don't have transportation. While all of these may actually prevent some Latino parents from being active in the school, in reality, many of these issues are not culturally related. The reasons that keep Latino parents out of the schools are primarily structural. How the schools

and parent involvement programs are organized determines whether Latino parents
are included and are able to participate or not. (20–21)

Perspectives from other educational scholars are aligned with Gaitan's position, but include that some Spanish-speaking parents do indeed recognize the
import of their involvement in schools and advocate for more parent-teacher
conferences and interactive workshops, as well as community partnerships.
These observations also affirm the belief that the cultural tradition of *familismo* centrally locates parents in their child's education, which can potentially
result in high academic outcomes.

A third dynamic linked to minimal parent participation is health issues.
As opposed to suburban or rural areas, researchers insist that urban, low-
income families are more likely to be subjected to substandard food, housing,
and medical care. Environmental issues like community violence, restricted
access to quality hospitals, and limited child care facilities play a decisive
role in how parents approach other facets of life.

Families from underprivileged communities are more often physically
sick or psychologically unable to meet the demands and expectations of
schools, given their day-to-day stress and anxiety. Decaying urban centers
can also leave low-income residents in a state of depression, isolation, and
mental paralysis. Without basic physiological and emotional needs being
met, families can struggle in a way that school professionals cannot see.
Although teachers may desire more parental involvement in schools, many
are fighting just to preserve their own sense of mental stability, as well as the
economic structure of their families.

With respect to one's psychological outlook, low self-esteem is yet another obstacle hindering parent participation. In addition to the harmful mental effects brought on by minimal basic needs, parents who were unsuccess-
ful, or had bad experiences in their schooling years, might still carry with
them a poor self-concept related to their education. The stress that schools
symbolize for these adults imbues them with a level of distrust that is difficult to get past. They recall the authoritarian teacher and feeling defenseless
as a student. In their adulthood, they may still feel powerless in the presence
of teachers and be reluctant to question their decisions. Others might take on
a more oppositional stance to their helplessness and become noninvolved as
a rebellious act.

Associated with hurtful schooling experiences, low-income parents might
imagine that a teacher could threaten their self-esteem at a school function
such as report card pick-up. The overuse of edspeak can distance parents in
these talks, making them feel that middle-class educators are patronizing
them or acting superior.

When parents feel that teachers are being judgmental, without intimately
knowing their child and the issues that they deal with, parents can become

quite sensitive and reactionary during these meetings. This response is typical in the preserving of one's self-esteem. Hence, as a way of sustaining this vital aspect of the self, parents will disconnect from teachers. This is not to say, however, that they will be uninvolved in their child's education at home, but rather that they will be less inclined to participate in organized and mandated school functions.

A final barrier is *cultural dissonance*. This phenomenon, linked to many of the racial and class differences above, is a feeling of conflict based on the cultural incompatibility between teachers, parents, and students. Teachers of dissimilar backgrounds may have limited knowledge of what parents and students go through on a daily basis, which might make them hard to reach.

White middle-class teachers, for instance, may not be acquainted with the cultures of working-class families of color and misinterpret their parenting behavior as "uninvolved." These teachers can also be led into making false assumptions about students of color based on their parents' lack of involvement and, in turn, can ignore these students or be more apt to impose sanctions upon them. This can very well lead to student hostility, as well as apathy, toward schooling.

When educators come with school-centered notions of what parents "should" be doing, they lead themselves into a series of mistakes: First, they dismiss the contributions that parents may be already making, but that are invisible to teachers inside the classroom. Second, they extend the rift between schools and homes by directly and indirectly communicating to parents "what counts" as involvement. Third, they can perpetuate the myth that low-income, or non-English-speaking, parents do not care about education. This simply is not the case.

In effect, there are other factors as to why students do not succeed in the school setting besides a perceived lack of parental involvement (e.g., low teacher expectations, culturally insignificant curriculum, students not understanding how they learn, and harsh disciplinary punishments laid down by the school). In chapter 5 we will discuss some of these issues closely as it relates to the classroom experiences of our participants.

Malissia

Malissia is eighteen years old and African-American. She sees herself as "smart and respectful." On the weekends, she likes to go to the movies and spend time with friends. Malissia's goals for the not-so-distant future are to graduate from high school and find employment. Further down the road, she wants to pursue law school. Malissia says that there is simultaneously one thing that she likes and dislikes about herself: "I don't change for nobody."

Family will always support you, no matter what. If you get up to something bad or if something happens, like if you lose someone that you truly love, they'll always be there for you. My grandma has played the most important role in my life. My mom was struggling and my daddy was in jail, so my grandma started taking care of me since I was five. Now, she's gone. She recently died and so basically my grandpa has taken over. But I thank my grandmother for that all she done for me. She always bought me clothes and everything. She's the one reason why I kept going to school. Even when I dropped out after eighth grade, because I was all into boys, she sat down and talked to me. She started reading the bible to me and talking about God and how my life was going to be better. She was like, "You don't want to be like your Daddy." I was like, "Okay, Grandma." So I went back to school. Ever since then, I've been going and haven't dropped out.

As we review some of the personal and societal barriers that confound parental involvement, we must also include the absence of primary parents—father and mother. In her own commentary, Malissia bears witness to the significance of her grandparents: "My grandma has played the most important role in my life. My mom was struggling and my daddy was in jail, so my grandma started taking care of me since I was five. . . . She's the one reason why I kept going to school." Malissia is indeed fortunate to have supportive grandparents step into her life and fulfill the roles of her absentee parents. It is distressing to ponder where Malissia would be in her life without the support that her grandparents provide.

Some of the reasons why grandparents become primary caregivers include: parent incarceration, substance abuse, child neglect and abandonment, teenage pregnancy, divorce, family violence, mental health problems, poverty, and death of a parent. Regardless of the severe circumstances that bring about their surrogate status, grandparents usually have the common goal of furnishing a stable and caring home environment for their grandchildren.

Becoming a surrogate can have substantial rewards for grandparents. Grandparenthood has been linked to the positive mental health and morale of elderly persons. Once again, they are in the cherished role of caregiver and in the company of family members. Interestingly enough, current research has found that a majority of grandparents favor a style of parenting that makes them less of a primary authority figure and more of a distant relative. The basis for this is that some elderly adults realize the incredible self-sacrifice that comes with grandparenthood. In many instances, these surrogates witness their economic resources, saved for their retirement years, being quickly drained in their efforts to meet the basic needs of their grandchildren.

According to the 2008 U.S. Census Bureau, 6.6 million youngsters were living in grandparent-headed households—a figure that has been increasing over the past twenty-five years. The same census reveals that out of the overall number of grandparent-headed households, grandmothers make up 1.6 million and grandfathers 932,000. While grandparents are progressively becoming "secondary parents," there are some factors that limit their full involvement in schools as well.

Going back to 2008 U.S. Census data, 1.5 million grandparents who were in the labor force were also responsible for most of the basic needs of grandchildren. Of this figure, 482,000 were living below the poverty level while still caring for their grandchildren. Insufficient financial income undeniably hinders grandparents' ability to find affordable housing and healthy living spaces for themselves, as well as their grandchildren, much less (or more) be engaged in school functions.

Grandparents also face the issue of legal guardianship. Children living with grandparents due to parental substance abuse problems are often still in the custody of their parents. In their absence, children, of course, must still attend school. Many districts, however, do not allow grandparents to enroll a child unless they are the legal guardians. Likewise, insurance companies do not permit grandparents to carry their grandchildren as dependents without formal custody. This makes it difficult to place grandchildren on health insurance policies. In order for grandparents to have total responsibility and authority, they have to go through a costly and time-consuming adoption and custody process.

A final factor that adds a degree of difficulty for grandparents' involvement with schools is the charge they can have over multiple grandchildren. Grandparents can find it exceptionally hard to monitor the day-in and day-out activities of several children, which can be exhausting. Further, children from different generations make it challenging for elderly surrogates to understand or appreciate their grandchildren's social and cultural differences. In these cases, grandparents may not be able to fully grasp why young people act in the manner they do and are also confused about how to discipline them.

Despite some of the challenges of grandparenthood, the weight and significance of their presence is key in the lives of young people living without a mom or a dad. As pointed out earlier, parent incarceration is just one reason why grandparents become surrogates. When working with urban youth, the authors have found that all too many of these young people have relatives who were either jailed or are presently incarcerated—some of these youngsters speak about their father as one. The quality of relationships between urban youth and their fathers is of the highest import. Malissia and Simone spoke about the absence of their fathers and what it has meant to them.

Malissia

> I had hatred for my daddy. I didn't like him. My daddy got out of jail when I was five. Next, like a couple of weeks later, he got locked back up. I mean, so it was basically in and out, in and out, in and out. I was sixteen when he got out the last time, like two years ago. I didn't even go by to see him. I didn't even want to see his face. I didn't want to say nothing to him period. I don't even talk to him now. I hate my daddy. He didn't have his act together. He wasn't acting the way a father supposed to act.

Simone

> Your mother cuddles with you. Your mother cares for you. If you have something wrong, she'll listen to you more than your father will. Your father will be more stern and he won't really listen, but your mother would. She'll care for you. She'll be there at all times. Me and my father—I thought he was supposed to do that. After he didn't, I felt that, if he was there, I probably would not have gotten pregnant because he would've been a father figure. He would have put that fear in me. Not the bad fear, but the good fear. Because of him being a man, he would tell me all the wrong things about boys. But because he wasn't really there I had to find out on my own and somewhat from my mother.

In their interviews, both Malissia and Simone showed a level of distress when talking about their fathers. Although their comments above moderately capture this, these young women indeed feel an enormous loss from their father's absence. The most recent data from the U.S. Census Bureau reports that approximately one in four children are living in homes where no father, biological or otherwise, is present. This figure disproportionately impacts Black children as barely over 60 percent (compared to 21 percent Hispanic and 17 percent White) live in single-parent households primarily headed by mothers.

When fathers are present in the lives of their children, the effects are clear. Research shows that highly involved fathers advance healthy childhood development in areas of cognitive ability, social competence, and emotional well-being—each may be negatively affected by a loss of time and care from a second parent or adult.

Research also indicates that children of nurturing fathers exhibit a higher level of self-esteem, improved school performance, greater intrinsic motivation to succeed, and stronger sexual identity and character. Children of highly involved fathers are also observed to have fewer psychological and behavioral problems and are less likely to become delinquent and engage in substance abuse or early sexual activities.

Additionally, fathers play an integral role in the financial support of the family. In the average two-parent home, the father's income makes up more than half. Yet fathers who earn low wages and experience high rates of unemployment often find it difficult to fulfill their parenting roles from a financial perspective. Noncustodial fathers who are low-income, unemployed, or incarcerated have the added obstacle of not being able to secure sufficient monetary assistance to pay for child support. This barrier subsequently leads many of these fathers into the kind of debt accumulation that pushes them to become negligent in fiscal and emotional responsibilities.

Studies on uninvolved or nonresident fathers and the reasons for their absence are sparse within the research literature. Much of what exists focuses on the negative consequences of divorce and the loss of household income to traditional, middle-class families. There is much that needs to be explored as to what long-term effects father absence has on adolescent, unmarried, and/or low-income mothers, with particular consideration to the organization and stability of the family unit, the child's overall development into adulthood, and the magnitude of the effect that the father's income or incarceration has on his involvement with both children and the mother.

Regarding incarceration, Malissia stated that her father was in and out of jail throughout much of her life. Jailed fathers obviously not only represent another obstacle to full parental involvement, but also a risk to healthy and enduring family ties. In 2007, parents confined to the U.S. prison system were mostly male at 92 percent.[6] More than four in ten fathers were Black, about two in ten were Latino, and three in nine were White. An estimated 1,559,200 children had a father in jail that same year—46 percent were children of African-American fathers.

Several factors dictate an incarcerated father's capacity to maintain a nurturing relationship with his children, as well as the continuance of his paternal rights. For one, the inability to provide reliable emotional and financial support of a child can render fathers powerless. This disposition, combined with feelings of shame and embarrassment, can cause imprisoned fathers to alienate themselves from their children, as well as other family members.

Another factor is the duration of conviction. In minimal sentences, fathers may receive parenting time or visitation. In harsher punishments, visitation can be limited and fathers might see the full termination of their paternal rights. Alternatively, there are cases where fathers who were highly involved in their child's life before confinement retain some level of custody, even if serving an extensive sentence. These fathers have the chance to maintain contact with their children and the mother, in spite of internment. In other cases, fathers can have paternal rights totally eliminated, regardless of their extensive participation. The courts base this judgment on the view that jailed fathers are in no position to participate in the decision making of the child.

Finally, paternal rights and family relationships can be jeopardized due to prison geography. Remote locations can make fathers virtually inaccessible. Custodial rights are gravely considered by the courts, in the interest of stability to the child, when fathers are not easily available. Also, family ties can be severely tested as fathers may have rare opportunities to see their children or the mother and offer them emotional support.

With respect to low-income and disadvantaged families, we do know that father absence makes the household more vulnerable to stress and poverty. Data on Black and Hispanic single-mother families show that limited access to resources and information about resources can create a cycle of relative family disorganization that is intergenerational and tremendously hard to break. The problems facing these families over an extended period of time, however, are not exclusively a function of poverty, but also a result of ineffectively implemented policies, flawed educational training, and racist and discriminatory practices within the labor market.

When a father is absent, the positive outcomes of his involvement can be inverted. Children and adolescents, devoid of a caring father figure, are theoretically denied a much needed model to assist them with personal and academic issues. The public discourse widely stresses the negative impact that father absence has on Black and Latino boys in particular. Young men of color are documented as reacting in antisocial ways in schools and communities as a result of not having early exposure to adult males who support them in developing healthy coping strategies and problem-solving skills.

For Black and Latina girls, the effects of father absence may not be completely dissimilar to the experiences of their male counterparts. Girls' emotional and academic development can equally be at risk when fathers are not around. Teachers and school counselors find identical levels of daughter resentment toward absent fathers, with the outcome of this anger observed in how girls respond to social and emotional situations. A hint of this is seen in Malissia's comment about the hatred she holds for her father, as well as in Simone's statement about the significant role her father might have played in her life: "I felt that, if he was there, I probably would not have gotten pregnant because he would've been a father figure. He would have put that fear in me."

In the face of father absenteeism, some evidence suggests that for Black and Hispanic families, depending on the cultural contexts, multiple family members can help improve the psychological functioning of youth without fathers. In some cases, these are men serving as "fictive" or "other" fathers who help supplement the absence of nonresident biological ones. They may be uncles, grandfathers, cousins, friends, teachers, coaches, mentors, stepfathers, or a dating interest of the mother.

As mentioned previously, the broader social network of family, for Latinos, is culturally termed *familismo* (or within research as *natural support systems).*[7] For African-Americans, the workings of family organization are referred to by scholars as *family communities.* This is defined as an assortment of related and nonrelated persons who collectively assume responsibility in rearing children. We see this most notably in Malissia's relationship with her grandparents. In either cultural community, youth are emotionally and financially supported by nonparental adults, who are committed to seeing them academically achieve and succeed in other aspects of life.

CLOSING COMMENTS AND RECOMMENDED RESOURCES

Urban public schools are by and large a middle-class enterprise that caters mostly to low-income and working-class families. For Black and Latino parents from these social class backgrounds, the stigmas attached to their noninvolvement emerge out of traditional school-perspective ideals of parent participation. Not only do these parents have to deal with personal problems outside of schools, but they also face the challenge of being stereotyped by school professionals—teachers, principals, psychologists, and counselors.

In order to genuinely see the lives of children and families of color, school professionals must be willing to step beyond narrow racial and social class orientations that are instilled with deficit-model beliefs that utterly blame parents for their child's educational failure. Unless practitioners work to expand their thinking and make learning environments inviting and trusting spaces, connections between schools and homes will continue to fray.

Rather than trying to engage families by using school-centered strategies, schools must become more parent-centered. As they do this, schools allow themselves to understand how parents of color are involved in their child's learning, which often takes place outside of school, where parents teach the 3 R's in everyday conversations or sometimes with actual instruction in the home. In other words, some parents represent educational resources. Yet these can be the same parents that can be labeled as "apathetic" or "not educated enough."

At the end of the day, finger-pointing at parents only misses the mark. School professionals must understand that the same things they want for their students, families also want for their children and more. Parents, like the ones of our participants above, are often involved in their child's education in ways that educators cannot see. With that, below are some ideas for building greater visions for school-home connections.

1. Open up the school doors to parents, not to "involve" them but to "engage" them. That is, as opposed to presenting parents with school opportunities based on some pre-established list of activities created by the school, parents and other members of the community can work collaboratively to develop endeavors that address the needs and concerns of that community. These may be, for example, parenting workshops, computer classes, employment advising, or social events.

2. Home visits may prove beneficial in helping professionals develop relationships with students and families, becoming more conscious of their out-of-school lives. For instance, teachers can learn which students have to work, need baby-sitting, require transportation, or actually have both parents actively present in the home.

3. Schools might connect with local churches as a way to engage parents in those spaces. For some African-American and Hispanic groups, the church represents an intimate resource. If educators can make themselves present in those spaces, then families may see school professionals as less detached and more congenial.

4. Schools should tap into natural support systems and family communities, which can be underutilized resources, especially when the focus is always on parents. In other words, if a mother or father is not available to be at the school for whatever reason, teachers or principals, with the consent of the guardian(s), can generate a list of other familial and nonfamilial members to call on for sharing information about the student or garnering family engagement in school-based activities.

Books

The Best Kept Secret: Single Black Fathers by Roberta L. Coles (2009/Rowman and Little-field).

Black Families at the Crossroads: Challenges and Prospects by Leanor Boulin Johnson and Robert Staples (2004/Jossey-Bass).

Building on Strengths: Language and Literacy in Latino Families and Communities by Ana Celia Zentella (2005/Teachers College Press).

The Essential Conversation: What Parents and Teachers Can Learn from Each Other by Sara Lawrence-Lightfoot (2004/Ballantine Books).

Hispanic Families at Risk: The New Economy, Work, and the Welfare State by Ronald J. Angel and Jacqueline L. Angel (2009/Springer).

The Power of Parents: A Critical Perspective of Bicultural Parent Involvement in Public Schools by Edward M. Olivos (2006/Peter Lang Publishing).

Preparing Educators to Involve Families: From Theory to Practice by editors Heather Bastow-Weiss, Holly Marie Kreider, M. Elena Lopez, and Celina M. Chatman-Nelson (2005/Sage Publications).

The Strengths of African American Families: Twenty-Five Years Later by Robert B. Hill (1999/University Press of America).

School, Family, and Community Partnerships: Your Handbook for Action by Joyce L. Epstein and Associates (2009/Corwin Press).

Articles

Critical race theory and ethnographies challenging the stereotypes: Latino families, schooling, resilience and resistance by Sofia Villenas and Donna Deyhle (2002/*Curriculum Inquiry* 29(4): 413–445).

Effects of family structure, family process, and father involvement on psychosocial outcomes among African American adolescents by Deborah A. Salem, Marc A. Zimmerman, and Paul C. Notaro (1998/*Family Relations* 47(4): 331–341).

Ethnic and cultural diversity in fathers' involvement: A racial/ethnic comparison of African American, Hispanic, and White fathers by John F. Toth Jr. (1999/*Youth and Society* 31(1): 76–99).

The impact of fathers' absence on African American adolescent gender role development by Jelani Mandara, Carolyn B. Murray, and Toya N. Joyner (2005/*Sex Roles* 53(3/4): 207–220).

Rethinking parent involvement: African American mothers construct their roles in the mathematics education of their children by Kara Jackson and Janine T. Remillard (2005/*School and Community Journal* 15(1): 51–73).

Websites and Organizations

Coalition for Community Schools (www.communityschools.org)is an association of national, state, and local organizations focused in areas of education (grades K–16), community planning and development, family support, and health and human services.

National Center for Fathering (www.fathers.com) works with more than one million dads per year through seminars and small-group training, assisting all kinds of fathers (e.g., biological, nonbiological, and grandfathers) with techniques and strategies for parenting.

Parental Information and Resource Centers (www.ed.gov) is funded by the U.S. Department of Education and designed to plan and execute parent involvement policies, activities, and programs that lead to student high academic achievement.

Parents as Teachers (www.parentsasteachers.org) is a resource site for parents, organizations, and professionals dedicated to successful early childhood outcomes.

Parents for Public Schools (www.parents4publicschools.com) is a national organization of community-based chapters that work with parents, involving them in public school advocacy and reform that impact school improvement and student achievement.

1. Hispanic family values mirror several of the general traits found in family resiliency models (e.g., *respetar a otros*—mutual respect in relationships; *compadrazgo*—strong ties between parents and extended family members like godparents; and *ser buen educado*—emphasis on proper behavior and discipline), but also includes *respeto*—respect for education and teachers.

2. Authentic assessment, as more than objective test measures (multiple choice or true and false responses), measures real-world knowledge and skills needed for success in adult life. Tasks generally include reading and writing, or otherwise literacy, abilities that resemble in- and out-of-school situations.

3. Detracking refers to reducing or eliminating tracked classrooms based on student grouping by abilities and having more heterogeneous classes with students from all ability levels.

4. Standards-based education is a school reform initiative that focuses on student mastery of defined curriculum standards. Standards-based education has been adopted by nearly every U.S. state and is the driving force behind local, state, and federal educational policies.

5. Gaitan, C. D. (2004). *Involving Latino Families in Schools: Raising Achievement through Home-School Partnerships.* Thousand Oaks, CA: Corwin Press.

6. Forty-eight percent of all mothers held in the prison system, in 2007, were White, 28 percent were Black, and 17 percent were Latina. Of the approximated 147,400 children with a mother in prison, about 45 percent had a White mother, compared with African-American children at 30 percent and Hispanic children at 19 percent.

7. In a report titled, *The Puerto Rican community and natural support systems: Implications for the education of children* (1992/Center on Families, Communities, Schools, and Children's Learning), author Melvin Delgado refers to "natural support systems" for Hispanics as extended family, community-based organizations, and neighborhood help groups that go beyond the short-term needs of finances.

Chapter Five

The Power of (Mis)Education

Education remains the key to both economic and political empowerment. —*Barbara Jordan*

Theories and goals of education don't matter a whit if you don't consider your students to be human beings. —*Lou Ann Walker*

We have a hunger of the mind which asks for knowledge of all around us, and the more we gain, the more is our desire; the more we see, the more we are capable of seeing. —*Maria Mitchell*

When most people use the term "urban education" it typically means the schooling of Black and Hispanic children. While it may indeed be that, particularly in a city like Chicago, where African-American and Latino students make up a large majority of all school children, the notion of urban education is nothing new.

Over 150 years ago, urban education was about schooling the first wave of post-Revolutionary immigrants from eastern and southern Europe—many of whom were poor and working-class. Educational reformers Henry Barnard and Horace Mann saw rising illiteracy, poverty, and violence taking place in cities like Boston, Philadelphia, and New York, and established compulsory schooling to educate the masses for the purpose of safeguarding America's existing social and moral fabric and growing industrialization.

Fast forward to 2010, we note that urban education is about more than social class; it's also about race—particularly given the disproportionate numbers of students of color attending city schools. Thus, when we use the term "urban education," it does, in fact, have a specific look to it. In this century, urban schools experience an array of daunting realities that often differ from suburban and rural schools—higher rates of teacher turnover and school closings, inadequate resources, truancy, overcrowded classrooms, limited parent participation, rigorous accountability measures, elevated levels of violence, and excessive policing.

The primary source for some of these issues is thought to arise from inequitable school funding that is directly tied to community economics, which, in most U.S. cities, is directly linked to race. The degree to which schools are financially supported plays a central role in how students' needs are met, as well as the resources provided to teachers to successfully prepare youth of color for a competitive global economy.

American schools are subsidized by three basic revenue streams: federal, state, and local property taxes. The state of Illinois, for example, relies heavily on local property taxes, which funds about 53 percent of all school expenditures. Over the past several years, however, Illinois only paid 36 percent of all school expenses—far below the national average of 50 percent. The remaining portion comes from federal aid in the form of No Child Left Behind (NCLB)[1] and other federal initiatives. Illinois's funding system, similar to many other states, perpetuates serious educational inequities as schools located in areas with few thriving businesses and low property values will accordingly have low per-pupil expenditures.

Unpacking inner-city economics further, youth of color living in poor communities endure many burdens. They may face limited access to extracurricular programs, as well as daily exposure to gun violence, gang rivalry, drug dealing, prostitution, and other harmful situations. Urban youth may also reside in deteriorating homes or in cramped quarters with numerous family members. The stress internalized by these conditions can make youngsters depressed and even hostile. The inevitable corollary is that students' temperament will find its way into classrooms and hallways, making students incredibly hard to reach and educators unable to only teach pedagogical content.

When teachers are underprepared to deal with students of color from impoverished areas, and the issues associated with their life circumstances, the challenges of teaching become magnified. The majority of students attending urban public schools nationwide are Black and Hispanic and low-income. The bulk of public school teachers, on the other hand, are White and from middle-class backgrounds.[2]

Being that these educators tend to be unaware of students' cultural communities and unable to appropriately read their behavior, what can result is cultural dissonance in teacher-student relationships. In some instances, educators stigmatize students and resolve (consciously or unconsciously) not to teach them, and students, feeling inept or mislabeled (real or perceived), choose to no longer learn. Educational scholars argue that the consequences of these severed relationships are observable in disproportionate rates of minority students dropping out, being suspended or expelled, and/or being referred for special education services.

The overrepresentation of Black and Hispanic students in special education often mirrors their overrepresentation in other deleterious categories such as dropout rates, low-track placements, suspensions and expulsions, and involvement with the juvenile justice system. Over the past several years and with the utilization of zero-tolerance policies in schools, African-American and Latino students have been widely documented as being suspended and expelled at higher rates than White, Asian/Pacific Islander, and American Indian/Alaskan Native students. Suspension and expulsion rates are reported as higher for males than for females. Black male students overall have the highest rates of suspension and expulsion of any other racial group.

In *Countering the Conspiracy to Destroy Black Boys*[3] (1995), Jawanza Kunjufu discusses the result of cultural dissonance in relation to African-American males:

> Female teachers, especially White ones, are integral in the development of Black boys in America. Since the *Brown vs. Topeka* case of 1954, desegregation has more than ever brought Black boys into contact with White females. In light of this, it can be noted that 83 percent of all elementary teachers are female. Black children only constitute 17 percent of all students but comprise 41 percent of all special education placements, primarily as Educable Mentally Retarded (EMR) and Behavioral Disorder (BD). Of the Black children placed in special education, 85 percent are boys. (83)

Essentially, U.S. public schools create expectations and evaluate results based on ideas, beliefs, and values generally accepted by the dominant culture of schools. Thus, curriculum and its outcomes are racialized in a way that can negatively impact those who are seen as culturally different and, in most cases, viewed as defiant. Cultural anthropologist John Ogbu referred to ethnic groups within this phenomenon as an *oppositional culture.*

Ogbu's theory basically posits that historically oppressed groups (e.g., African-Americans, Puerto Ricans, and Mexican-Americans in the Southwest) resist schooling and other White-controlled arenas because they have a history of subjugation with Whites and mainstream institutions. Although Ogbu's theory elucidates and even predicts that students of color will challenge schooling in general, it primarily indicates that their resistance stems from their exploited status. As such, their opposition will be stronger with White teachers than with Black or Hispanic ones.

The key drawback to Ogbu's theory is that while it stresses one's racial history, its attention to cultural dissonance places little value on those dynamics occurring in and outside of schools. It overlooks, for example, reasons as to why children of color are optimistic and hopeful in their early schooling years, but face a decline as they move into adolescence. The explanation for this, beyond Ogbu's assertions, is that by the time students of color enter into their teenage years they begin to perceive their educational efforts as undervalued within society. That is, they gain the awareness of other minority groups' social adversity, as well as their own, within a structure and system of assumed social mobility.

Rather than solely relying on Ogbu's theory of oppositional culture, we should also recognize that the schooling experience itself can diminish students' enthusiasm and love for learning. Given that schools can fail to authentically connect with minority students' culture, while simultaneously insisting they change it, noncompliance to the process of schooling is probable, especially for those students who value and are highly attuned with their cultural identity.

The dissonance that some Black and Hispanic students feel toward school is not just a matter of cultural incongruence with teacher beliefs and biased curriculum, but also of ideas generated by the larger society. Controlled representations send Black and Hispanic youth unhealthy messages about their self-worth and value, before they ever enter school doors. These pervasive messages are vibrant in how low-income youth of color are treated by police officers, their inability to find fair employment, their vilification in media, and the lack of resources and helping hands in their communities.

The schools young folks of color attend mirror and perpetuate these harsh social dynamics in a variety of ways. Thus, students of color can expect to find, even when not looking, the same social and economic deterrents in schools that they observe in their own communities. Is it any wonder why they become disenchanted with schooling, as well as with other mainstream social institutions?

Since their inception, public schools have functioned to maintain an obedient citizenry, preserve the status quo, and inculcate traditional American values. Although these goals are more implicit in today's operation of schools, curriculum and disciplinary codes of conduct still represent the primary methods by which the above functions are carried out.

In the case of African-American, Chicana, and Puerto Rican females, it is clear as to why some might challenge these covert schooling objectives, given that they are aware of their predetermined status as "Other" as White culture is seen as the acceptable "norm." The sociocultural myopia of teachers and administrators works to shape these students into "proper" girls; that is, those who are well-mannered, compliant, and "act White."[4]

This shaping process routinely demands their silence and the domination of their bodies, while never actually considering their cultural identities (e.g., their history, their language, and the ways in which they interact with others). To that end, some Black and Hispanic females refuse to become "invisible" within the mainstream as they have much to say about living in a world where social justice is illusory. This is demonstrated by those who choose to protect their identities by speaking their mind, being assertive, or even electing to disconnect themselves from institutionalized education.

When adolescent females of color determinedly exercise their voice in classrooms and hallways, they can be perceived as egregious and rowdy and, at times, disciplined for it. Yet, from another perspective, their outward expressions could also be interpreted as a sharp interrogation of ideals, concepts, and morals that they do not agree with or fully grasp.

As mentioned in other sections of this book, the adolescent mind is becoming gradually aware of how broader social dynamics function. While some of these girls may not be able to articulate the politics of the world like some adults, they nevertheless become perceptive of concealed institutional values and are naturally compelled to question them.

Labeling females of color as ignorant, subversive, unintelligent, or "Alpha," as a result of their actions, would be an incorrect cultural assumption that not only encumbers our understanding of these youngsters, but also of the contextual ambiguity surrounding femininity. In other words, their voice may not purely be opposition to femaleness in and of itself, but rather a challenge to dominant sociocultural expectations of gender that they view as false or incomplete.

Even so, the institutional dilemma that these girls face is one where if they adhere to silencing, they become complicit in maintaining conventional models of female dependency and docility. Yet, if they remain assertive, then they fall into the artificial image of an unscholarly or disobedient student. Regrettably, in order for some to be taken seriously, they must learn to acquiesce and give up their voice.

In this chapter, the authors explore two primary themes surrounding school life, based upon the data collected from our participants: *the importance of being educated* and *student treatment in schools*. These themes helped to organize student perspectives around the personal significance that education holds for them and the in-school experiences that influence how they negotiate classroom life and develop their own internal sense of agency. We begin with the first theme.

"IT'S PEOPLE LIKE YOU"

Angelica

I like education because it keeps my mind going and going. It keeps me active, so I don't have to do nothing stupid out in the street.

Simone

Education to me is the key to everything basically. I have a child and I feel that I have to set my standards higher than I would normally do. I want my child to get into a good school, to compete with somebody, to compete with me. You know, like get that good GPA, the good grades, and go to the good college and stuff like that. So I feel that education is something that everyone should be willing to do because it benefits you in the long run.

Mya

Most teenage girls drop out of school when they get pregnant, you know, and they don't go back. They stop thinking about their education because they're pregnant, but some of them go back to school like me. That's a good thing to do because if you don't go back to school that's going to make you feel low. That's going to make your child think, "Oh, my mom didn't finish school or my dad didn't finish school. I'm going to be just like them." So, I mean, it's good to have an education. It's good to graduate. Even though there's still people who got their diploma but don't go to college and end up working at a McDonald's or somewhere, it don't matter. Education will help you get through life.

Being educated for countless girls and young women worldwide is about creating greater agency and access for oneself. In nearly every corner of the world, girls and women still encounter vast inequities around education, nutrition, health, and economic opportunities within the labor force. In those spaces where families endure overwhelming poverty, the assurance of education is that one can gain the power to improve their life.

For the young women above, education offers them this promise and that they have the potential to make individual change. Education for Angelica, for example, keeps her "active" and out of the streets. For Simone, it serves as a vehicle for her and her child in securing "long run" benefits such as attending a "good college." For Mya, the completion of schooling helps to build self-esteem, while also modeling a positive parent figure.

As we have discussed in previous chapters, teenage parenthood has a lasting effect on how girls and young women relate to schooling. When the added responsibilities of parenting arise, formal education can often take a back seat. In fact, pregnant adolescents are more likely to drop out of high school with only about one-third going on to graduate.

The penalties for these female dropouts is that they will make significantly lower wages, experience higher rates of unemployment, have less access to health care, and depend on government support in far greater frequency than their male peers. For those teen mothers who acquire a diploma, we still find that almost 80 percent will have a low annual income and rely on welfare at some point in their lives.

In spite of these bleak realities, Mya and Simone clearly see the necessity of schooling beyond themselves and toward the multiple long-term advantages for their children. The resilient nature of these young mothers in staying committed to education, as opposed to dropping out, becomes essential in breaking cycles of poverty and limited educational achievement within families.

As reported by the National Women's Law Center in 2007, dropout is indeed a "multi-generational problem" (10).

Not only are students who drop out of school likely to suffer the personal consequences of dropping out, such as lower lifetime income and worse overall health, but they are also more likely to see their own children drop out of school and suffer the same consequences. (10)

While teenage pregnancy has been correlated with lower socioeconomic status, it perpetuates the above cycle as educational attainment goes hand-in-hand with level of income. Research shows that teens whose parents have lower levels of schooling are more likely to engage in precarious sexual behavior and almost certainly become pregnant. Yet it is their pregnancy that can lead to their exiting of schools without a sufficient education to secure a well-paying job to support them and their child.

The idea that children of teen dropouts will potentially replicate the educational and employment levels of their parents is confounding to ponder. Thus, it is decisively apparent how the education of these young women is critical in expanding their abilities and choices in order to reduce the likelihood that they will live in poverty.

No question, educational and supportive services influence outcomes for pregnant and parenting teens and their children. Without reliable access to social and economic capital, adolescent moms can face dismal circumstances. Therefore, it is vital that school curriculum not only support the traditional high school academics, but also the emotional and psychological elements of early childbearing for those teens that experience this life situation.

With the understanding that there are those students who after becoming parents resign to the vision that they are unable to achieve the same academic and professional goals of their nonparent peers, we must create educational spaces that offset their doubts and fears. In doing so, we supply them with better opportunities to possess the long-term socioeconomic status that they imagined and desired before motherhood.

Even though teenage pregnancy is considered the leading factor as to why girls decide to vacate the school institution, it is not the only one. Other reasons that have been correlated with female dropout are poor grades, feeling unsafe in school, undue disciplinary measures, limited family involvement in schools, home responsibilities, employment demands, and substance abuse.

Race, class, and gender are rarely extrapolated as part of these additional correlates within the research literature, even though one could easily surmise how an issue such as feeling unsafe in school might relate to gender as female students face greater instances of sexual harassment than males. With regard to poor grades, there is a plethora of literature by educational scholars who examine the relationship between biased curriculum and low teacher expectations, which can lead to students' academic disengagement.

With recent studies showing that the female dropout rate has been mounting over the past several years, the leading question that arises is: What schooling experiences force low-income girls of color away from their education, particularly as they understand its connection to social mobility?

Yet, when students from poor, urban neighborhoods decide to ultimately abandon the school building, perhaps it is not their education that they are walking out on, but rather the nature and process of institutionalized schooling that presents them with subpar academic content, culturally incompetent faculty and staff, and school settings that fail to differ from their communities.

For the young women above, education is used to denote schooling. While these young people have learned the importance of education and its capacity to keep their "mind going and going," conceivably it is formal education that precludes them from meeting their full potential. In the next section, we look at what our participants had to say about their *treatment in schools* and their relationships with teachers.

Halle

I'm the type of person that can trigger off really fast. Like, if a teacher tells me to be quiet and listen, I can't because it's hard for me to take some of the side comments that come with it. Like, I had a White teacher and she said to me, "It's people like you." I asked her what she meant and she couldn't even explain it, but I already knew what she meant. On my first day of school, she started automatically picking on me. On my third day of school, I got suspended because she lied and said I pushed her. But I would never put my hands on any teacher because I have respect for my elders and I'm not like that. Anyway, she caused me to miss a whole bunch of days of school and I ended up slacking off and falling behind. When I did try to get caught up, it wasn't as easy as I thought it would be. That teacher just caused me a lot of unnecessary problems.

Mya

White teachers shouldn't stereotype us because of what they see in videos. They shouldn't be like, "She looks like this girl off this video. She got her hair like that Beyoncé. She must be like this or like that." At my school, there might be a few who do judge you like that because they just down you. But apparently not all of them because most are willing to help you get through school. I mean, teachers should understand us more because they was our age and they know how it was, and also because everybody's different. Teachers gotta ask how we feel and we gotta tell them not to judge us.

Malissia

Everybody got their rights. We're not back in the old days when they [African-Americans] used to just be quiet when White people would tell them to be quiet and tell them do this or do that. I mean we're teenagers. Of course, we're going to be loud, we're going to do what we want, we're going to do this and do that, we're going to do our homework whenever we want or maybe not at all. I'm like, they [White teachers] can't tell us what to do. I feel that White teachers be trying to take our rights. That's just how I feel.

Beyond the monetary inequities that shortchange the educational experiences of students of color is the discrimination they face in schools. The most widely examined racial phenomenon, within the context of classrooms and student achievement, is the matching of White teachers with Black and Hispanic students.

As the research literature points out, teacher expectations of minority students around academics and behavior are negatively influenced by a Eurocentric ideological framework. From this standpoint, African-American and Hispanic students' conduct and learning styles are not just divergent from White students' in a culturally subjective manner, but further interrupt what the teacher is trying to achieve. When this is the mind-set, teachers may be all too swift to eliminate the presumed "classroom disruption" from sight in the form of suspension or expulsion.

The cultural and racial bias that educators bring into classrooms is exampled in the above student narratives. Halle and Mya are both objectified by their teachers through such expressions as "It's people like you" and "She looks like this girl off this video." While these young women clearly speak to racial encounters, we observe that Mya and Malissia also associate their experience with age differences between them and their teachers.

Despite their references to *ageism* and *adultism*, racial connotations are more prominent in their experiences by virtue of that fact that they claim: "White teachers shouldn't stereotype us because of what they see in videos" (Mya) and "We're not back in the old days when they [African-Americans] used to just be quiet when White people would tell them to be quiet and tell them do this or do that" (Malissia).

No question, these student comments reveal that, like teachers, students also bring biased cultural attitudes into schools and classrooms. This is seen in how Mya and Malissia use a broad stroke in painting their White teachers.

The distinction, however, is the hierarchical relationships that exist within traditional classroom structures where teachers are sovereign (possessing nearly all of the power) and students are subordinate (having virtually no power at all).

In this arrangement, it is the adults who hold major influence and control in classrooms and it is their decisions that can detrimentally affect the academic outcomes and life chances of minority students. When cultural misimpressions undergird this hierarchy, educators are acting in racist ways that they themselves may be unconscious of, yet students easily recognize in daily lessons and interactions.

Race, ethnicity, color of skin, and the cultural manner in which one speaks and carries oneself are all represented in imagery and schema whereby teachers draw judgments—even racist judgments. Stereotyping within this context is a prevailing force that threatens student academic achievement, as well as psychological well-being.

Whether conscious or unconscious of them, the biased attitudes that teachers possess become highly problematic when they cast students into a racialized "box" and subject them to all of the habits, judgments, and expectations of an entire ethnic group. When educators teach in this manner, learning ultimately becomes oppressive and alienating. And, as research points out, this adds to student disengagement from academics, their ensuing underachievement, and their overall disdain with schooling.

The overt and covert stereotypes suffered by our participants above are described in the literature as *racial micro-aggressions*. These often subtle or nonverbal insults are communicated through rude looks, gestures, and attitudes in everyday teacher exchanges toward students of color. Over time, students can become sensitive to these tactics and feel their resiliency being tested.

Racial micro-aggressions, in effect, emerge from teachers' culturally biased frames of reference that are powerfully conditioned by a deficit model way of thinking that locates the causes of low academic achievement, poor behavior, and social exclusion in the deficits of minority students and their families. The repeated outcome is the placing of students into pathologized social categories such as learning disorder, cognitively delayed, behavioral disorder, oppositional defiant disorder, criminally minded, and sexually deviant.

The fundamental problem with the deficit model is that it overlooks entrenched structural factors such as race, class, and gender that have significant effects on the lives of young people of color. This skewed epistemological framework, in the context of schools, holds that minority students (especially those who do not fit within established teacher expectations) do not already possess the required skills, knowledge, and attitudes needed to learn and to achieve.

Rather than furnishing these young folks with first-rate education, combined with tenderness and patience, teachers chalk them up to being "difficult," "hard to reach," and in dire need of being "fixed" through special education services or correctional facilities. Suffice it to say, this manner of thinking works as a forceful agent in cutting off students of color from both academic and life successes.

Simone

If you're black, they expect you to be loud and loud black girls are perceived as troublemakers.

For instance, when I was a freshman, my principal told me one day, "Don't ever grow up to be like them. They're standing around, they're loud, they're snickering, and they're talking about other people." He was referring to these seniors hanging out in the hallway and the bell hadn't even rung yet. But I looked up to them because they were where I wanted to be. I didn't look up to them because they were loud or ghetto. I just wanted to make it to my senior year and graduate from high school.

When I think about it, I really don't know what "loud" means anyway. I think I'm loud, but other people don't think so. I think teachers and principals see loud as being stupid, but you can be loud and still be an A student. When teachers see that you're loud, they try to change you. They try to change you from what you're used to. Maybe it's for the better, but it might not be something that you want to do. So when you don't do it, teachers look past you or don't bother with you anymore because you're still hanging with that crowd, but you're making good grades.

The racialized gendered "Other" that Simone talks about is that of the "loud Black girl." This specific stereotype transcends learning environments and is culturally ascribed to Black people in general. In the context of schools, however, the interpretation of Black girls as being loud, in one sense, emerges from the perception that these students are "ghetto" and "ignorant."

In another sense, "loudness" is seen as a high level of assertiveness and independence that is not the "norm" for children and adolescents. Both interpretations unequivocally speak to hegemonic frames of reference held by educators who have very little awareness of their racial biases, as well as individual and cultural variances within the interface of race, class, gender, and even age.

Over the past twenty years, much has been written about minority students' struggle to maintain their academic achievement and positive racial identity inside of schools. Educational scholars have recognized that while Black and Hispanic learners are quite academically capable, they tend to minimize their intellectual abilities and underachieve as a form of resistance to the process of schooling. Their opposition is, in part, due to the perception that they must choose between their scholastic attainment and racial identity as incompatibility exists between their home and school cultures.

Scholars Signithia Fordham and John Ogbu[5] assert that if other Black students see acceptance of school norms as a denial of Black identity, then the high achiever may be perceived as "acting White." Like Fordham and Ogbu, Angela Valenzuela[6] also refers to schooling as a "subtractive process" for Mexican-American youth as it strips them of vital social and cultural resources that render them susceptible to educational failure. For Valenzuela, Chicano students' opposition to learning is about subjection and a fear of losing one's identity (e.g., the co-optation of language) within a system that is believed to hold promise and opportunities in one's life.

Other researchers have argued that student resistance is not rebellion without cause. Indeed, there are a host of reasons as to why students challenge their schooling experiences. These can range anywhere from their perception of inadequate curriculum to excessive testing, and from disliking teachers to simply having a bad day. Yet, within the context of understanding students of color, verbal loudness, while associated with unruliness, can be a means of sustaining identity and self-agency in a domain of subordinated social status and forced compliance.

For females of color, specifically Black girls, who are raised in a cultural and familial setting where voice is elemental to one's culture (e.g., its use within Christian or Evangelical churches), protecting identity entails resisting silence. This is a delicate balance that we see in the life of Simone. She states, "I think teachers and principals see loud as being stupid, but you can be loud and still be an A student . . . you're still hanging with that crowd, but you're making good grades."

Aside from how Simone successfully navigates her schooling experience, "loud" female students are frowned upon and are cautioned by educators not to be around. The institutional norms that pervade hallways and classrooms consider verbal loudness as one of the most disdained student behaviors, especially when shown by girls. Being "loud," combined with being Black or Latina, situates these girls beneath the racialized labels of "licentious," "amoral," "bitch," "grown," and, as Simone points out, "troublemaker."

Pigmentation, however, does not correlate with being "loud." In effect, "loudness" is a social construct that bears its roots and power within an established patriarchal society. From a cultural perspective, Black females—historically and presently—have been portrayed as the near opposite in nature to White females. If White women are gentle, quiet, innocent, and feminine, then Black women are rough, loud, libidinous, and masculine.

As discussed in chapter 2, media plays an integral role in perpetuating this dichotomy through its representations of African-American women as the "Mammy," "Jezebel," and "Diva." The construction and propagation of these controlled images become a part of the unconscious public psyche, which destructively impacts how teachers see and interact with Black female students. This is evidenced in all of the young women's comments above.

Similarly, when "loud" Latinas challenge the gender expectation of being silent and submissive, they can easily fall into categories of immoral and insubordinate females. Yet it is their cultural belief system, as well as teacher perception, that compels some to remain quiet and passive—something reinforced by educators, media, and family members—which further stereotypes their classroom behaviors. Some of these girls and young women recognize that if they acquiesce to established gender pressures, they not only narrow their academic outlook, but they also constrict their vision of life opportunities.

In schools, the assertive Latina or Black girl can be relentlessly silenced through punishment and sanctions. Educators use silencing as a method to control classrooms and to squeeze students into proverbial boxes. The outcome for some girls of color is that they can become virtual ghosts. If they make good grades, it comes at the cost of losing their persona. If they play the game of the "acceptable" or "scholarly" student, then they may very well have to give up their voice in order to do so.

What is interesting about Simone is that she is able to safeguard her persona, in spite of what her teachers expect. She maintains friends and certain individual behaviors that, while speaking to a racial stereotype, do not totally represent her. According to Simone, she remains assertive, but is still taken seriously as a scholar. Her experience is all the more reason to recognize individual variances within cultures.

As a caveat to the above, the authors believe that the reason Simone is able to preserve her racial identity and secure good grades is because of her social geography. She attends a fairly small alternative school comprised of all low-income African-American and Hispanic students. Even though it is a learning environment where curriculum still mainly reflects Eurocentric values, the pressure to "act White" and to be traditionally feminine is not as intense as perhaps a school where White, middle-class students would be the majority.

CLOSING COMMENTS AND RECOMMENDED RESOURCES

What does it mean to educate urban youth effectively in public schools? As has been discussed throughout this book, cities have a distinct set of characteristics that, in many ways, differ from suburban or rural settings. Public school students (mostly folk of color and working class) bring rich experiences into the classroom that may be considerably unique from teachers and students from other cultural backgrounds and locations. To effectively reach and educate urban children and adolescents, school professionals must make a genuine effort to become acquainted with the multiple cultures, skill sets, community lives, and the knowledge base that young people accumulate outside of school.

In meeting this end, educators should take the opportunity to explore the "funds of knowledge" that students possess as a way to develop and organize curriculum that speak to students' present life and future goals. Teachers can tap into this knowledge base by working alongside students (and their families) to devise lesson plans and activities that urban youth view as socially and culturally relevant. Out of this, young people can gain a direct understanding of how schooling and education benefit them in a real and convincing way.

Before and during this process, the authors highly suggest that school professionals, particularly those unfamiliar with urban youth of color, must reflect on their attitudes, beliefs, expectations, and fears about the students they will be working with. The values that educators carry with them into schools and classrooms can be somewhat contradictory from those of students. Much of the incompatibility that exists between student and teacher values can lead practitioners into misperceiving, mistreating, miseducating, and misdiagnosing young people of color.

Obviously, the deeply engrained beliefs that practitioners hold cannot be transformed overnight. Thus, in order to expand their mind-set, and thereby become more competent in their profession, educators should continually take part in personal and cultural stories with students and families, expose themselves to readings that relate to today's multicultural and multilinguistic world, and engage in diversity training in-services that assist professionals in critically examining matters of race, ethnicity, class, gender, and systemic inequality, and how these issues can intensely impact student learning and behavior.

Outside of teacher training, the effective education of urban youth requires that public schools incorporate services and programs that function to diminish substantial socioeconomic barriers that youth and their families encounter daily. For instance, schools can network with community-based organizations that offer an array of services such as employment assistance, financial management, marriage and family counseling, health services, tutoring, mentoring, child care, and sex education programs.

In addition to community-based partnerships, some schools have the capacity to offer students adaptable educational curriculum that provide students with access to academic options within the school system. Examples include: flexible class times (e.g., late morning or early evening classes); high-quality, critical-thinking assignments as opposed to a total reliance on standardized tests; year-round schooling where instruction can take place with greater consistency; and the use of cooperative learning groups where students can work collaboratively on projects that promote high-order thinking and application to "real-world" concepts. Below is a list of further resources that school professionals can utilize.

Books

Construction Sites: Excavating Race, Class, and Gender among Urban Youth edited by Lois Weis and Michelle Fine (2000/Teachers College Press).
Courageous Conversations About Race by Glenn E. Singleton and Curtis Linton (2006/Corwin Press).
Cultural Diversity and Education: Foundations, Curriculum and Teaching by James A. Banks (2006/Pearson Publishing).
The Dreamkeepers: Successful Teachers of African American Children by Gloria Ladson Billings (1994/ Jossey-Bass Publishers).
Educating Teachers for Diversity: Seeing with a Cultural Eye by Jacqueline Jordan Irvine (2003/Teachers College Press).
The Mis-education of the Negro by Carter G. Woodson (2008/Classic House Books).
Multicultural Practices of Effective Teachers of Urban Students: Successfully Educating African American and Latino Students in Urban Schools by Cloetta Veney (2010/Lambert Academic Publishing).
Narrowing the Achievement Gap: Strategies for Educating Latino, Black, and Asian Students edited by Susan J. Paik and Herbert J. Walberg (2009/Springer).
Persistent Inequality: Contemporary Realities in the Education of Undocumented Latina/o Students by Maria Pabon Lopez and Gerardo A. Lopez (2009/Routledge).
The Power of Their Ideas: Lessons for America from a Small School in Harlem by Deborah Meier (1995/Beacon Press).
A White Teacher Talks about Race by Julie Landsman (2009/Rowman and Littlefield).

Articles

Black adolescent racial identity and respectability by Garrett Albert Duncan and Henrika McCoy (2007/*Negro Educational Review* 58(1/2): 35–48).
The color of caring: Race and the implementation of educational reform by Jean A. Patterson, Jenny Gordon, and Paula Groves Price (2008/*Educational Foundations* 22(3/4): 97–116).
From opposition to engagement: Lessons from high achieving African American students by Greg Wiggan (2007/*The Urban Review* 40(4): 317–349).
I (don't) hate school: Revisiting oppositional culture theory of Blacks' resistance to schooling by Angel L. Harris (2006/Social Forces, v. 85(2), pp. 797-831).
The impact of White teachers on the academic achievement of Black students: An exploratory qualitative analysis by Bruce Douglas, Chance W. Lewis, Adrian Douglas, Malcolm Earl Scott, and Dorothy Garrison-Wade (2008/*Educational Foundations* 22(1/2): 47–62).
The silencing of Latino student "voice": Puerto Rican and Mexican narratives in eighth grade and high school by Pamela Anne Quiroz (2001/*Anthropology and Education Quarterly* v. 32(3): 326–351).
When race matters: Teachers' evaluation of students' classroom behavior by Douglas B. Downey and Shana Pribesh (2004/*Sociology of Education* 77(4): 267–282).

Websites and Organizations

Classroom Diversity (www.classroomdiversity.com) has an exhaustive list of classroom teaching methods, management activities, lesson plans, and teaching skills aimed at diversity instruction.
Edchange (www.edchange.org) provides teacher resources, curriculum, and classroom activities that focus on social justice and humane education in schools and classrooms.

Teen Diversophy (www.teendiversophy.com) has an association of educators, administrators, and consultants who offer a range of expertise in best practices around educating young people on diversity issues.

Wilderdom (www.wilderdom.com) is a unique website offering educators in- and out-of-school activities centered on peace education, multicultural education, and experiential learning.

1. The Elementary and Secondary Education Act (ESEA) of 1965 was amended and reauthorized in 2002 as the No Child Left Behind Act (NCLB). The four main principles, or pillars, under NCLB are: stronger accountability for school results, greater local school district control and spending flexibility, an emphasis on scientific research and curriculum, and increased choices for parents.

2. In 2008–2009, White, middle-class females constituted just over 80 percent of all elementary school teachers and roughly 60 percent at the secondary level. Seven percent of teachers in the United States are African-American and 8 percent are Hispanic.

3. Kunjufu, J. (1995). *Countering the Conspiracy to Destroy Black Boys*. Chicago: African American Images.

4. To "act White" means to participate in a range of Eurocentric social practices and ways of being such as speaking Standard English; making good grades; listening to classical or rock music; reading White authors; attending plays, operas, or ballets; studying in the library; visiting museums; or going camping. For students of color taking part in such behaviors can lead to their educational and academic enhancement, yet result in their social alienation.

5. See: Fordham, S., & Ogbu, J. (1986). Black students' school success: Coping with the "burden of 'acting white,'" *Urban Review* 18:176–206.

6. See: Valenzuela, A. (1999). *Subtractive Schooling: U.S.-Mexican Youth and the Politics of Caring*. New York: SUNY.

Chapter Six

Is There a Place for Me?

Calling all sisters. Calling all righteous sisters. Calling all women. To steal away to our secret place. Have a meeting face to face. Look at the facts and determine our pace. Calling all women. *—Ruby Dee*

One of the most valuable things we can do to heal one another is listen to each other's stories. *—Rebecca Falls*

Given the variety of topics broached by the young women in this book, the authors now move toward constructing a space where their concerns can be genuinely addressed both individually and collectively. Depending on the exigency of student issues, the space we are conceptualizing can render itself in the form of either a school- or community-based program. In order to assist as many students as needed and within a single setting, we recommend a school-based program that focuses on youth mentoring.

The following sections illustrate some of the social, emotional, and intellectual elements that we feel are necessary for creating a successful *school-based mentoring* (SBM) program for girls and young women of color. While our proposed SBM program is, for the most part, discussed within the context of the school environment, much of what is stated can be directly translated into a community-based framework.

Mentoring is characteristically thought of as a relationship where an older and wiser individual shares knowledge and insights with a younger, less experienced person. It can occur one-on-one between two nonrelated individuals (e.g., teacher and student, student and student, supervisor and staff member) or between relatives (e.g., parents and children, older family members and younger ones). It can also take place within a collective, where one or more mentors work with a group of mentees.

In its practice, mentoring is sometimes formally arranged in organizations of employment and educational institutions or informally between people who casually form a kinship. Whichever way it proceeds, mentoring ideally involves a person consistently supporting, informing, guiding, and nurturing another.

SBM programs that focus on students' emotional and physical well-being often become a site for helping young folks deal with personal matters that are not adequately addressed during the school day. The general structure for most SBM programs finds students meeting in a group forum and engaging in social activities and dialoguing with peers and adults about important life issues.

The group dynamic enables mentors to reach large numbers of young folks at one time and offer them immediate advocacy, counsel, and relief from stressful situations. Where programs face a shortage of volunteer or paid mentors, group formats help to offset adult unavailability. In these cases, you will observe, for example, two to three mentors working with a cluster of ten to fifteen students at once.

Beyond the effective use of space, time, and human resources, group mentoring has other notable functions. For adolescents, peer groups are highly valued personal outlets. Although the general opinion of peer circles is that they have negative influences on young people, they do offer a number of positive outcomes:

- Supportive peers and friends help to maintain social and emotional well-being;
- Interacting with positive peers and friends enhances self-esteem;
- Ethics are tested and evaluated in peer groups, further enhancing moral reasoning;
- Emotional exchanges aid in teaching expression of feelings;
- Gender-role behaviors and sexual attitudes are adopted and shaped.

Peer groups can provide youth of color with all of the utilities above, but are also considered to be legitimate and valuable sources of knowledge for them, especially when they perceive schools as institutions that undervalue their culture, language, and belief systems. For youth of color, the peer group can be an incredible information base that aids in building resiliency, most notably in the absence of adult role models. Within these community circles, students of color share similar fears, conflicts, and resolutions, while simultaneously validating cultural experiences. It is the above qualities of peer groups that should be incorporated into this conceptual SBM program.

Given the emotional aspects that the group mentoring space engenders, the most critical elements to be found within it must be *safety* and *trust*. Youth and adults participating in this space need to feel that their physical and psychological welfare is not threatened. Although absolute safety may not be likely, the SBM setting should be as consistently safe as possible. Communicating the value of respect for all program participants is one way to initially establish a protective space.

In creating a safe space, students can jointly develop a list of rules that meet the safety needs and concerns for all those involved. While developing rules can sometimes come off as mundane or trite to students, they should be made aware of the value of them, as rules help to encourage and maintain structure and stability.

Inextricably linked to safety is trust. Trust becomes vital to those spaces where young people are engaged in processing and revealing their emotions. Students will not openly disclose personal issues in a group setting, if they do not trust those around them. Without trust, young people will remain distant, guarded, and unwilling to be receptive to any advice that one may impart. Even adults can remain closed off if they themselves do not feel a degree of trust.

Trust has a number of dimensions that range from the corporeal (I trust that I will not be physically attacked by another person) to the emotional (I trust that I will not have my feelings hurt), and from the psychological (I trust that no one will mock my ideas or malign my identity) to the spiritual (I trust that my spirit will not be abused by negative words or actions of others). If the space that is being created does not strive to be one of integrity and care, then trust-building will fail.

Safety and trust are prime elements in creating a space for girls. Like some of the young women in this book, students can go their entire school day, as well as their out-of-school time, not being able to trust anyone around them. By no means does a student want to feel that at any given moment somebody can walk up to them and physically or verbally attack them. Thus, in building an SBM program, mentors and mentees must work together in fostering an atmosphere where respect and appreciation are not static. Rather, they are real; they are genuine feelings that radiate throughout the classroom and are reciprocated by those willing to participate in a shared space.

As previously stated, one way to establish a trusting and safe environment is to communicate to all participants the essential nature of each. While verbalizing this indeed helps, actions speak much louder than words. In many cases, it is the actions of adults that serve as leading examples for our young people. How they act, as well as how they respond to situations, must be modeled through mentors.

Youth are constantly confronted by teachers, principals, police officers, parents, even mentors, who fail to take into consideration the intricate and delicate lives of children and adolescents. As opposed to being embraced by some of these adults, youngsters can be mistreated or ignored by them. The harsh reality, for some youth, is that such maltreatment begins early in their lives and by the time they enter adolescence, they hold an intense distrust toward adults. This disposition, while warranted, compels many youth to keep their emotions bottled up, disconnect from school and society, and refuse to accept any support that an adult may offer.

Developing a safe and trusting SBM environment requires that adults become more aware of the in- and out-of-school lives of students. Safety and trust are partly constructed on seeing students in all of their fullness and humanity—their strengths, their weaknesses, their kindness, and their cruelty—and accepting them without condition.

In those moments where young people stress the most opposition or behave the most enraged, adults must continue to show them that they care and are there for them. In this instance, safety and trust are beyond rhetoric—they become tangible and internalized. Adults help to make such concepts authentic by opposing apathy and exhibiting true care and concern. When this ensues, there is greater probability that children and adolescents will open up their lives and be receptive to a space that is designed to genuinely support them.

Once again, adults must be willing to become more attuned with students' personal lives, if they are truly determined to create a place where youth have the opportunity to feel safe around others, develop trusting relationships, and speak out about their issues without being judged, admonished, or infantilized. Likewise, adults must also be willing to remove themselves out of the traditional hierarchical arrangement that situates them at the top and youth at the bottom of social and organizational structures, as in schools and classrooms.

In *Mentoring Young Men of Color: Meeting the Needs of African American and Latino Students* (2006),[1] Hall presents a concept called *the Act of Removal*. It is a pedagogical practice for adults attempting to develop horizontal relationships with students.

> While it is sometimes easy for us to confuse authority with omnipotence, we must try to break away from the "my way or highway" mentality that is pervasive in teaching and instruction. Instead, we must make the attempt to subordinate ourselves and come to see schools and classrooms as ethical sites, where students can be the creators of their own learning experience and teachers as the facilitators of that knowledge. This is the *Act of Removal*. It is a process whereby classrooms become less dominated by adult authority and more youth-centered and focused. The objective is to construct learning environments that foster youth empowerment, free expression, self-discipline and self-respect. With these notions in the forefront of our educative practices, student resistance to classroom learning can be minimized. (24–25)

In theory and in practice, the Act of Removal seeks to construct partnerships between youth and adults through power-sharing. From one perspective, adults learn to beless robotic and more human; less authoritarian and more just; less closed and more open to the needs and concerns of students.

From another perspective, youth become less defiant as their own identities and experiences are now heard and validated. Where before young people were silenced and dictated to, the Act of Removal helps to level the classroom "playing field" and advance an atmosphere of communal dialogue, respect, and dignity. Here, mentoring begins with the understanding that although the student participants are marginalized and underserved members of society, they too have a cadre of rich assets that can be used to access their self-empowerment.

Within the context of an all-girl SBM program, utilizing the Act of Removal is essential. Often girls lack the institutional space, inhabited by open-minded adults, where they can express their beliefs, rightfully argue their perspective, and seek impartial advocacy. School and home settings are filled with conformist ideologies and expectations for females—how they should behave and the sexual roles that they should subsume. African-American and Latina girls' rejection of traditional beliefs have created the perception of gender defiance, which has lead to increased methods for their silencing.

In practice, the Act of Removal constructs a place for girls to bond with peers and voice their thoughts on sexism, classism, and racism, which may not be tolerated, empathized, or critically examined within everyday social locations like schools and communities. Equally, the Act of Removal requires that adult mentors "take a step back, close their mouths, and open their ears to the range of thoughts and feelings being expressed by their mentees" (Hall 2006, 27).

In this context, girls' voices become the center of dialogue rather than narratives at the margins of discourse. As individual voices flourish, program participants begin to see one another as fully human, eroding misleading perceptions and prejudices, as well as the stereotypical imagery that surrounds girls of color (e.g., at-risk, deviant, gangbanger, welfare mom, or ghetto, etc.). The next section presents a more precise description of mentoring and the expected role of mentors as viewed by the authors and some of our student participants.

"JUST LIKE MY BIG SISTERS"

Fontessa

Fontessa is African-American, eighteen years old, and a senior on the verge of graduation. She is tall and slender and admits to being a tomboy, with most of her friends being boys. Fontessa will be heading off to college in the autumn. She plans to enter into the same university that her high school principal attended. From our interview, she stands out as a natural leader and undeniably has the aura of being a "big sister."

When I think of mentoring, I think of help, encouragement, strength, and building your self-esteem. I think it's getting to know people better and figuring them out because everybody is going through something different. When you first start out, they [mentors] get to know you, and they won't have a prejudged idea of you, and they'll just try to help you based off of what they know and they try and become your friend. They let you know that they won't just give up on you or be disappointed in you because they're the ones that supposed to help you and try to teach you what you're capable of doing.

My dad's not around like my mom is, and she's pretty cool and says I can talk to her about anything. But there are just some things I don't want to talk to her about because I don't want her to feel like, "Oh, my baby girl," or I don't want her to look at me different, or try to force stricter rules on me because she feels I might go down another path, so sometimes you need a mentor.

My mentors talked to me about my problems and I was able to talk to them. They were just like my big sisters, and I was comfortable because even though I talked to them about certain things that might have disappointed them, they still helped me, they still smiled. They still cared. They didn't just give up on me.

Antoinette

Antoinette is African-American and a seventeen-year-old high school junior who is plus size with a big smile. During our interview she was shy and appeared nervous. One of the major things that stood out about Antoinette was how many times she mentioned losing friends and being able to talk to her own mentors about the situation. Antoinette emphasized that girls needed female mentors who have the understanding of what it's like to be a girl.

When referring to the word mentoring, it's like getting help from somebody or somebody that you can talk to and feel comfortable with sharing yourself with them and having somebody that relates to exactly or somewhat of what you are going through. Me personally, I have very supportive parents, my mother, father, stepfather, stepmom, whatever. But I still feel that you need a mentor at the same time because they tell me what I need to do and what I have to do to get where I want to be.

Mentors help us out and things, and any problems that we have, they are like the type of people that you can talk to any one of them. Sometimes you may have just that one person that you feel comfortable talking to. It's been times when I was just like I want to quit, and my mentors were just encouraging me saying, "Just don't quit," you know, "we going to get this straight." They there for me.

Lloyd

Lloyd is African-American and a seventeen-year-old senior who stands out as "boy crazy." In fact, the name she selected as her pseudonym is the actual name of a popular African-American male R&B singer who she dreams of marrying. In her interview, Lloyd spoke with an air of confidence that transcended her heavy-framed, bookish glasses and shiny lip gloss. Indeed, she was very convincing about her positions. This fall she will be attending a local university.

> A mentor should help you with whatever area you need help in. Even though teenagers have a lot of the same issues, a lot of the stuff isn't the same. A lot of kids feel like that can't talk to their parents about things and stuff and there should be someone you can talk to about that kind of stuff because you never know what will happen.
>
> Sometimes your guidance counselor isn't always the best person to go to. At big schools, your guidance counselor is not going to know everybody personally and that's always important. So having a mentor helps because a mentor has to know you personally. I mean, that's the best way for them to help you solve your problems or give you any kind of advice.

In accordance with the Act of Removal, adults and youth must work in horizontal relationships as opposed to conventional hierarchical ones. In schools and communities, youth can be faced with adults who regularly prescribe to them narrow and moralistic ways of being. These adultism tactics seek to "fix" young people through the inculcation of values pre-established by the status quo. In mentorship practices, adults need to turn away from this conservative and antiquated paradigm as it reflects a deficit model approach.

The mentorship model proposed here is designed to curb giving mentees constant directives and prescriptions based on where adults believe they ought to be, instead of meeting them where they are presently. Most adolescents already have a sense of values and morals. Although some youth may need more guidance than others and others may require more time to explore social mores, mentors must concentrate on the promise of young people and not their perceived pathologies as the deficit model suggests.

Children and adolescents already have ideas of what they desire out of life, but often need social, emotional, and intellectual support to attain it. Rather than dictating to youngsters, adults should listen to their lives, become more responsive to the choices that they are making, and help them in interpreting their own issues and concerns. This is youth mentoring in both theory and praxis.

As is evidenced in the three narratives above, young people possess an instinctive, as well as an experiential, grasp of how mentoring should occur.

Fontessa, Antoinette, and Lloyd all speak of mentors as preferably being supportive, nonjudgmental, and respectful of one's personal life in and outside of school. According to these adolescents, mentors should assist youth in navigating social relationships by being receptive to any personal problems revealed during counsel.

These students also valued those mentors who were able to take emotional responses out of their advice and continue to be compassionate, in spite of the choices a young person had made. We observe this in Fontessa's commentary: "They let you know that they won't just give up on you or be disappointed in you because they're the ones that supposed to help you and try to teach you what you're capable of doing." In their efforts to uncover the potential young people hold, mentors should communicate numerous options, multiple doorways that expand their mind and not narrow their thinking.

More than any other time during human development, adolescence marks a period when young people consciously and unconsciously search for values and beliefs that differentiate from those established during childhood. Young people want to hear what others have to say with respect to politics, religion, sex, morals, and other areas of social life. They also want to express their ideas and perspectives that have been formed over time. The objective is for the individual to freely adopt those viewpoints that are agreeable and to discard those which are not.

With this is mind, mentors should offer their standpoint without automatically imposing their standards or ethics. This is part and parcel of creating a safe and trusting mentor-mentee relationship where mentors, as Antoinette asserts, are "big sisters, and I was comfortable because even though I talked to them about certain things that might have disappointed them, they still helped me, they still smiled. They still cared. They didn't just give up on me."

In order for mentors to become that beacon of support and guidance that the young women above describe and that all youngsters need, they must be able to suspend, at least for a moment, their individual lens. The reality for some youngsters may be in stark contrast to that of mentors. Their culture, their personal values, and how they handle day-to-day situations may be something that mentors cannot easily grasp or empathize with. Nonetheless, mentors should take themselves out of the center, as the Act of Removal recommends, and open their hearts and minds to the lives of struggling youth. It is hearing their stories that can better prepare mentors in effectively serving those mentees who are bearing harsh judgments from teachers, peers, and family members.

When adult mentors work to see beyond their own framework, mentoring relationships can be as constructive as the young women above attest to. Genuinely listening to the lived experiences of mentees informs mentors not only of where youth have been and where they hope to go, but also of what they socially and culturally value. These personal stories can guide mentors in assisting mentees in ways where youth are able to interpret and resolve their issues themselves, based on their own reality and not exclusively that of others. This progressively moves away from societal proscriptions and ultimately toward developing individual agency.

In her interview, Antoinette also made the point that female mentors are essential in connecting with girls. While the authors certainly feel that male mentors can work with female mentees and offer them a male perspective on relationships and parenting, schooling and employment, it is best that female mentors play the most integral and visible role in program planning and execution. The intrinsic understanding of how gender operates in society or in one's personal life provides the sexes with undeniable commonalities. Just as men bond with boys around issues of manhood, women also connect with girls around matters associated with womanhood.

Female mentors can express to mentees personal narratives about their journey from girlhood to womanhood. Aspects of womanhood related to biological changes, questions around sexuality and relationships, and gender oppression (to name a few) are detailed and embedded in the life experiences of women—the kind of sexualized and gendered circumstances that males really are not privy to.

If sensitive discussions around sexual intercourse, child abuse, or pregnancy should arise, then girls and young women will undoubtedly require boundaries that males cannot cross. This is paramount to developing a safe and trusting environment where voice is free. Moreover, as an all-girls SBM program will most likely draw on female-centered activities and curriculum, it is necessary to have female mentors available who can provide honest and reliable information that girls can see themselves in and be inspired by.

Simply having female mentors for girls, however, is not enough. Just as the authors believe that educators and counselors need to undergo diversity training, so too do mentors, particularly those whose life experiences and frames of reference do not reflect that of low-income Black or Latina females. As mentioned in the closing section of chapter 5, mentors, like teachers, may need to come face-to-face with their underlying expectations and assumptions of young people who are culturally different than themselves.

In the context of the girls featured in this book, genuinely mentoring them through the Act of Removal requires an understanding of the urban and personal issues that they face daily. As such, diversity training must involve mentors in heightening their critical consciousness of not only race, class, and gender, but also of sexual orientation, religious affiliation, child and adolescent development, as well as urban issues such as gentrification, gang violence, and concentrated poverty.

Mentorship, like teaching, involves adults connecting with students not necessarily in a sympathetic manner, but rather in a way that excites and compels young people to critically reflect on their life and to constructively transform it as they see fit. In meeting this end, let us now turn to a three-strand SBM curriculum framework that may best serve teenage girls of color.

Angelica

> If I was creating a program for girls, I would take them out like on Wednesdays and Fridays—those are good days to go out. Take them to the movies or go out to eat or go out to an arcade because it would take their mind off of things. Some of us girls go through a lot, you know. Inside we're hurting and some of us just keep it in and you don't realize what we're going through.

Toni

> Girls need a space to breathe, talk, and let out all the stress they're holding in. We need to have yoga classes and get massages. Just even therapy sessions—an hour or something to talk about our problems like dealing with home and the streets, having kids, and everyday things that society doesn't see. We need to talk about how some women degrade themselves and society mostly looks at women like sex objects. Like, when a girl gets hurt by a guy, she's going to talk to her girl about it because we're sensitive and stuff. So we just need to talk about it.

The central idea that emerges out of Angelica and Toni's narratives is the need for young women to engage in activities where they can voice emotions that have been internalized throughout the day. While both students offer us such examples as going to the movies, participating in yoga, or having massages as positive cathartic activities, the heart of what they want is a place and time to "take their mind off of things" [Angelica] and "to breathe, talk, and let out all the stress they're holding in" [Toni]. This is "voice," and in line with their responses, *self-expression* represents the first curricular strand of our proposed SBM program.

Self-expression—body, oral, or written—is unveiling one's thoughts, a sense of self and purpose. African-American, Chicana, and Puerto Rican girls experiencing stressful situations in school and/or at home may use unhealthy coping strategies (e.g., substance abuse, fighting, alienation) to avoid dealing with their issues. As more than simple utterance, self-expression invites girls and young women into a safe space where they have the power to express their ideas and bond with others, revealing previously hidden or unshared emotions. An indication of this is found in Toni's response: "When a girl gets hurt by a guy, she's going to talk to her girl about it because we're sensitive and stuff."

Beyond talking with one another, however, self-expression can be reflected through multiple art forms—journaling, poetry, spoken word, hip-hop, storytelling, song, and dance. Such portals can assist girls and young women in expressing their identities and externalizing personal problems. Art is a therapeutic process. It puts us in touch with our senses and allows us to see ourselves and others as fully human.

When girls reject, or are denied, the use of their senses, they can fall into depression, isolation, substance abuse, and even violence, particularly if such destructive manifestations saturate their school and community surroundings. Through art, voice becomes metaphorical, providing a window into the multiple life worlds of others. Girls and young women, who believe that no one recognizes their pain and struggle, undoubtedly must have this form of self-expression.

The next curricular element of our SBM program emerges from a critical pedagogical framework that encourages students to examine, interrogate, and reflect upon their world. In institutionalized settings such as schools, students, predominantly from subordinate groups, are often not allowed to validate their problems, resulting in feelings of disempowerment and alienation. However, this second curriculum strand seeks to engage mentees and mentors in *critical dialogue*,[2] where they can begin to problematize taken-for-granted social realities, expose unequal power relations and institutional values, as well as consider real possibilities for individual and social change.

Here, voice becomes less about the articulation of one's emotional or personal status, and centers more on intently confronting hegemonic matrixes of thought within schools and society. This aspect of voice functions to challenge the tension between dominant forms of discourse and the knowledge and cultural base of the individual.

For African-American and Latina females, critical dialogue is vital in helping them explore and comprehend the multifaceted ways in which identity politics (e.g., race, class, ethnicity, and gender) intersect and influence their personal lives. For example, in chapter 2, the authors discussed how various media outlets propagate stereotypical images of women of color. These representations, no doubt, have ideological and political aims that serve to socially construct females of color, leading to their stereotyping and potential mistreatment and misperception in schools and society.

When genuinely practiced, critical dialogue enhances the mentoring experience of girls of color as it supports them in "breaking their silence" and questioning the strong relationship between institutional power and their own knowledge and realities. The fundamental query that mentees and mentors must repeatedly ask themselves is, "Why is that?"

Critical dialogue broadens the minds of girls, unearthing within them the personal power to not only accept or reject societal scripts, but also to consciously understand why they are doing it. In this process, mentees can develop their own unique identity and perspective separate from artificially constructed images that do not accurately portray who they are or desire to be.

Hence, before our girls enter into a premature sexual act, before they perpetrate an excessive level of violence, before they abandon their education, they must be involved in rethinking their own thinking and authoring their own world, which by doing so, can present them with choices they never knew they had. Being heard and becoming vibrant agents in countering the knowledge and realities that are perpetuated about females of color places our girls in better positions of defining themselves as active—not passive—participants in the world around them.

Even though critical dialogue may not automatically rouse mentees to become civically active in their communities, it does hold the potential for building reflexive spaces where, after acquiring insight into deep-rooted structural factors such as gender exploitation and oppression, mentees can begin to feel encouraged to play a role in change efforts based on their own contexts. Hence, our third and final SBM strand is *youth activism*. It functions to authentically engage mentees in personal and social transformation.

For the authors, youth activist interventions and activities are primarily student-initiated, student-directed, and inherently focused on meeting the needs and issues of mentees. Mentors, of course, play integral roles as facilitators in assisting mentees with planning and accessing resources. Approaches within this strand include: organizing and conducting youth forums; serving on school boards alongside community leaders; working collaboratively with mentors or teachers to design curriculum; directing school- and/or community-based research projects; and planning political rallies and protests.

The key aspect of youth activism is that it is not meant to be a feel-good activity designed to placate students. Rather, it should genuinely function to challenge young folks to change their surroundings and themselves. As has been stated throughout the pages of this book, low-income African-American and Latina girls are extremely marginalized, if not altogether absent from our political and economic radars. Thus, youth activism can be used to construct a community-based forum that places substantial awareness and weight on real-life issues that Black and Hispanic females have to deal with daily.

Our girls are more resilient than media and society gives them credit for and they have much to say about life in society. As such, mentors and mentees must defy current educational policies that endorse subservience. Through this third strand, SBM programs can pull girls and young women of color out of "invisibility," initiate community conversations, and inform adults of the concerns around their existence.

If the voices of the participants in this book parallel concerns that might be discussed at a public forum, then what we as educators, parents, politicians, and mentors should walk away with is a greater sense of urgency in needing to confound the cycle of poverty that is rapidly inflating Black and Hispanic female statistics around teenage motherhood, school dropout and violence, and incarceration. Perhaps we might also leave with a deeper desire to act in the best interest of advancing and sustaining policies and programs that will safeguard the self-determination, well-being, and personal power of these young women, from prenatal all the way into adulthood.

CLOSING COMMENTS AND RECOMMENDED RESOURCES

If schools are truly service institutions, then we must organize them appropriately to address the needs, issues, and concerns of those who are entering their doors, carrying a host of emotional and psychological issues that obstruct their learning. We cannot expect young people to leave their problems at the doorsteps of schools. They indeed bring them inside with them. Therefore, we must, with all immediacy, create spaces and times for youth to vent and reorganize their thoughts in order to promote constructive thinking, learning, and living.

One cannot easily jump into learning if the mind is obfuscated by serious life issues that are not being addressed by schools or communities. Students then, quite appropriately, ask themselves: "What does this assignment have to do with my life and how does it help me presently?" While many young women accept the notion that education is key to a prosperous life, its road may be too long and winding for some of them to endure.

Developing a school-based mentoring program is just one strategy that schools can use to assist academically struggling females of color with more pressing life issues. The three strands presented here give potential programs ideas for activating girls and young women around such issues as racial and economic injustice, gender oppression, castigatory immigration and welfare policies, high-quality education, and liberation from violence. By creating spaces of multiple discourses, we can engage girls and young women of color in deconstructing these concepts, as well as other ones.

The general principle guiding our SBM program is helping girls and young women, from underprivileged urban areas, increase their personal power and life options. The advantage of having numerous choices is often a taken-for-granted privilege. In some cultural spaces, however, where choices or opportunities are limited on a day-to-day basis, the ability to create them can be an amazingly triumphant feeling.

Even so, this sense of empowerment and agency has to be supported by social policies that make options, as well as access to options, less of the onus of a school-based mentoring program and more of the responsibility of political institutions. For the young women that our SBM program is designed for, having choices should not be their struggle; it should be their undeniable human right.

Books

The Art of Critical Pedagogy: Possibilities for Moving from Theory to Practice in Urban Schools by Jeffrey M. Duncan-Andrade (2008/Peter Lang Publishing).

Educating Our Black Children: New Directions and Radical Approaches edited by Richard Majors (2001/Routledge).

Education for Critical Consciousness by Paulo Freire (2005/Continuum International Publishing Group).

Learning Power: Organizing for Education and Justice by Jeannie Oakes and John Rogers with Martin Lipton (2006/Teachers College Press).

Mentoring Children and Adolescents: A Guide to the Issues by Maureen A. Buckley and Sandra Hundley Zimmermann (2003/Praeger).

Teaching Critical Thinking: Practical Wisdom by bell hooks (2009/Routledge).

Working With Latino Youth: Culture, Development, and Context by Joan D. Koss-Chioino and Luis A. Vargas (1999/Jossey-Bass).

Articles

"The beauty walk, this ain't my topic": Learning about critical inquiry with adolescent girls by Kimberly L. Oliver and Rosary Lalik (2004/*Journal of Curriculum Studies* 36(5): 555–586).

Critical race theory, Latino critical theory, and critical race-gendered epistemologies: Recognizing students of color as holders and creators of knowledge by Dolores Delgado Bernal (2002/*Qualitative Inquiry* 8(1): 105–126).

Identifying best practices in civic education: Lessons from the Student Voices Program by Lauren Feldman, Josh Pasek, Daniel Romer, and Kathleen Hall Jamieson (2007/*American Journal of Education* 114: 75–100).

Investigating urban community needs: Service learning from a social justice perspective by Carol Wiechman Maybach (1996/*Education and Urban Society* 28(2): 224–236).

Participation in structured youth programs: Why ethnic minority urban youth choose to participate—or not to participate by Daniel F. Perkins, Lynne M. Borden, Francisco A. Villarruel, Annelise Carlton-Hug, Margaret R. Stone, and Joanne G. Keith (2007/*Youth and Society* 38: 420–442).

There are children here: Service learning for social justice by Marilynne Boyle-Baise and James Langford (2004/*Equity and Excellence in Education* 37: 55–66).

Websites and Organizations

Black Butterflies (www.blackbutterfliesonline.org) is a national youth-centered girls program that works with African-American girls and young women on issues of self-efficacy, self-esteem, body image, financial growth, healthy relationships, and college preparation.

The Mentor Network (www.thementornetwork.com) was founded in 1989 and is a national network of local community-based services for children and adults with physical and cognitive disabilities.

Mentoring USA (www.mentoringusa.org) is a New York City–based nonprofit that works to build meaningful relationships with youth and mentors, using the one-on-one model.

The National Mentoring Partnership (www.mentoring.org) is a national organization that promotes youth advocacy, as well as serving as a resource for mentors and mentoring initiatives worldwide. This organization in particular supplies information and support for individuals looking to create, manage, operate, and evaluate a mentoring program.

The R.E.A.L. Youth Program (www.realprogram.org), operating out of Chicago, uses a school-based mentoring model to assist children and adolescents in developing critical thinking and effective communication skills needed for life-long learning and success both in- and out-of-school.

1. Hall, H. R. (2006). *Mentoring Young Men of Color: Meeting the Needs of African American and Latino Students.* Lanham, Maryland: Rowman & Littlefield.

2. The liberatory philosophy of Brazilian educator Paulo Freire has substantially influenced critical dialogue. In Freire's notion of "problem-posing" education, the teacher-student dichotomy becomes obscure as both participants evolve into critical investigators of a world constantly shifting rather than remaining fixed. Critical dialogue, guided by methods for social analysis and the contestation of oppression, begins with the revealing of personal experiences and moving toward a shared understanding.

Chapter Seven

Conclusion

Don't be a marshmallow. Walk the street with us into history. Get off the sidewalk. Stop being vegetables. Work for Justice. —*Dolores Huerta*

Nobody's free until everybody's free. —*Fannie Lou Hamer*

The young women featured in this book offer us a glimpse into some of the everyday issues they contend with around school, family, and community life. Their words, at the center of this text, reveal how they construct and deconstruct meaning, interpret the world, and navigate their space within it. Their voices advance a more complete picture of who they are beyond the stigmas of "at-risk," "delinquent," "ghetto," or "baby's momma." What is more, they present us with insight into how they counter ethnic and gender stereotypes, oppose the dominant culture, and continue to be self-motivated and resilient in the face of severe social expectations and gender demands.

These young women's words rise to explain their existence, revealing and illuminating informed perspectives that, in their daily lives, often go unshared, masked, or obscured. Bringing the voices of these adolescents to the forefront of educational discourse enables broader public circles to see these adolescent women more clearly and to become more responsive to their individual needs, issues, and concerns. Their narratives of identity further help us to become more conscious of the multiple realities that they experience, progressively moving us away from misperceptions and false judgments.

Seldom are we presented with literature that accentuates the promise that young people of color possess. Much of what has been documented, regrettably, focuses on pathology. The knowledge of self and of culture expressed by our participants, however, acts as a viably constructive force in opposing myopic social perceptions of African-American, Chicana, and Puerto Rican teenage girls.

It is our hope that through these student commentaries, the attraction to deficit models, to "blame the victim" for her problems, becomes less tempting. As an alternative, individuals learn to push themselves to look deeply at social policies that ignore institutional discrimination and neglect, which produce and intensify many of the stressors experienced by the young women here (e.g., school dropout, teenage pregnancy, gang violence, physical and emotional abuse).

In reflecting on our time with the participants, the authors realize that these students navigate experiences that continuously have a bearing on their resilient natures. Despite the tremendous fortitude that they possess in managing their schooling, employment, family, and how they are represented and treated by the larger society, their resilience can certainly be tested. Without support of familial and/or nonfamilial members, it can be quite difficult to cope with the stress of limited access to a living wage, lack of quality child and health care, violence in schools and in homes, as well as shrinking social spaces where they can speak their minds and find real-life strategies to advance their social and economic conditions.

One of the ways in which we can help sustain the resiliency of the young women in this book, and others like them, is to work with them in fortifying—and in some cases rebuilding—positive attitudes about themselves. Recognizing that attitude is an aspect of identity, it follows that by building positive attitudes (e.g., optimism and self-assuredness) they can further achieve a sense of direction and personal coherence needed in successful identity formation and in life.

A strong, healthy attitude and self-image equips girls and young women for dealing with conflict that exists within and around them. Consequently, schools and other societal institutions must develop policies and curricula that focus on creating an authentic sense of care in classrooms and community spaces that foster prosocial behaviors, student agency, and economic independence. By creating such spaces of advocacy, we support females of color, who are enduring frustrated, overwhelming circumstances, in seeing multiple choices that can reshape their world.

Additionally, meeting the issues and concerns of African-American, Chicana, and Puerto Rican adolescent girls obliges us to understand various dimensions of human development interwoven into race, gender, and class. When girls of color act out in classrooms, their behavior is often seen as characteristic of their race, yet antithetical to their gender. Thus, the penalty that ensues is sadly based on external appearances.

If race is not viewed as a factor, then girls of color can be enveloped into another category—one that depicts *all* adolescents as angry, rebellious, violent, or confused. This exaggerated notion only encumbers our ability to see teens as individuals from different cultural communities and at different developmental milestones.

For educators, policy makers, parents, and community members, it is essential that we steer clear of popularized and inaccurate representations of girls of color. We must recognize that they, as all young people, have a strong desire to be successful, to feel loved, to be respected, to manifest their dreams, to be heard, and to be understood not purely as "inner-city youth," but as *youth*.

In meeting this end, we as a society and a global community must adjust our cultural lenses. We must come to the real understanding that while individuals have diverse needs and have to make decisions based upon those needs, we should all, in any circumstance, be viewed as nothing less than fully human.

Below are some closing thoughts from some of the young women who contributed to this book. They wanted this section titled "Words of Wisdom." It is their advice to other girls and young women who may be going through similar circumstances as their own.

WORDS OF WISDOM

Angelica

Don't be smoking or drinking because that makes you old. Stay in school, graduate, go to college, see more new things, go out of state, go to different countries, and meet new people.

Halle

Don't ever give up. Go with your first thought and stay strong.

Lapita

Don't give up. There's gonna be a lot of good times and a lot of bad, awful times, but don't give up on yourself. Just don't give up.

Malissia

You're going to make it regardless. Just keep on pushing and you're going to make it. Just keep on climbing that mountain and you going to make it to the top.

Mira

Stay encouraged. Encourage yourself, stay motivated—don't let nobody throw you off-track because they made you mad. Don't let anybody throw you off-track because they trying to do it on purpose.

Mya

You're gonna go through whatever it is that you gotta go through. Don't worry about what people say about you. You gonna go through stuff—that's life.

Nikki

Don't be negative, think positive. And when you think positive, you get positive back. You gonna have struggles, you gonna have storms, but after every storm there is sunshine. So be prepared for better days.

Shanny

Keep God first and keep your head up. Don't pay so much attention to what other people think about you and expect from you. You're only one person. You can only do what you can do.

Simone

Stay positive and go for what you're looking for.

Toni

Don't be naïve. Don't let a guy tell you what you can and cannot do. Don't let no one control you. Live a long life.

Glossary

Language can be lost and found in translation, depending upon who is making the meaning. For readers, words can be pleasant and inviting or exclusionary and arcane. Expressions can be modern and hip one minute and passé and politically incorrect the next. We offer this glossary to clarify some terms used in this book and also to preserve many of the critical ideas presented within it—ideas that we hope will not be lost in translation.

Access: The right to enter and to make use of resources within or produced by societal institutions, whether public or private. Access can be influenced by both economic and social status. For instance, lower-class groups may have difficulty acquiring access to traditionally exclusionary institutions and their resources. Conversely, upper- or middle-class groups may find gaining access to working-class institutions and communities an equally arduous task.

Adultism: The oppression of young people by adults, whereby all adults are considered superior in all skills and virtues to all children and adolescents.

Ageism: Conscious or unconscious discrimination of persons because of their age.

Alternative school: An educational setting with curriculum and teaching methods that are nontraditional or distinctive from mainstream schools. This type of school is intended to assist students who have been expelled from mainstream schools, are returning dropouts with minimal credits and/or below average reading skills, or struggle financially. While alternative schools tend to have a much smaller student body than traditional schools, many still lack essential resources.

Black womanhood: A concept of womanhood based on the historical, economic, political, and social experiences of African-American women. Distinct from Euro-American notions of womanhood, this view defines and validates the experiences of Black women within U.S. society and takes into consideration issues of slavery, emancipation, discrimination, motherhood, sexuality, and division of labor.

Bling-bling (or bling): Flashy, often extravagant, jewelry such as diamond (also termed "ice") rings and earrings, bracelets, watches, and gold or silver medallions. Bling has also come to include car rims, clothing, and even removable teeth caps encrusted with jewels.

Body image: A general term referring to how an individual perceives and evaluates their physical appearance. An element of body image is *body dissatisfaction*, which essentially is a negative assessment one has of their body or an aspect of it.

Charter school: A school that receives funding from either private or public entities or a combination of both. While they are still held to state and national accountability standards, they typically have the freedom to develop their own policies and regulations that may differ from traditional public schools. Charters can be established by corporations or nonprofit organizations, as well as parents or teachers.

Class (or social class): The hierarchical classification of individuals and groups in society based on prestige garnered primarily through financial success and the accumulation of wealth. The five basic social classes, in ascending order, are as follows: (1) Underclass; (2) Lower class; (3) Working class; (4) Middle class; (5) Upper class.

Code of the Street: Developed and enforced by urban street culture, "the Code" amounts to a set of informal rules that dictate public behavior, such as violence. The rules within the Code inform persons of attitudes and responses that they should have if challenged. "Streets" refers to rules and norms that are usually in opposition to mainstream society. Typically, wherever the Code of the Streets functions, members of that community know the penalties for breaking its rules. For instance, "snitching" is a severe breach of the Code, which can result in the bodily injury, or even death, of the "snitcher."

Edspeak: Specialized words or phrases used by professionals within the educational field.

Femininity and Masculinity: These terms are rooted in social prescriptions (i.e., gender) rather than the biological structuring of femaleness or maleness (i.e., sex chromosomes). Cultural groups essentially determine what female or male means (e.g., submissive versus domineering or fragile versus tough). Within each category, individuals construct a sense of self, as well as an expectation for their respective sex. (See: *gender identity, gender role,* and *gender stereotype.*)

Gender confluence: The adoption of certain traits, qualities, and characteristics of the opposite sex while maintaining many roles and scripts of one's own gender identity. For example, girls, typically thought of as being quiet and sensitive, may exhibit classic masculine behaviors of rowdiness and toughness, but still perceive themselves as largely feminine. Confluence of masculine and feminine attributes can be a natural way of being for some individuals, while creating disharmony for others due to powerful societal expectations of gender roles and behaviors.

Gender divergence: When an individual adopts the traits, behaviors, and characteristics of the opposite sex, giving up their gender identity and the roles that are inherent with it. Homosexuality is an example of this.

Gender identity: The belief that one belongs to the sex of birth.

Gender role: Sexual or gender behavior that is customary within one's culture. While social judgments on gender roles are changing, there still exist strict opinions on the roles of boys and girls and women and men.

Gender stereotype: Generalized ideas about the characteristics and behaviors associated with being female or male, which typically involves societal labels (e.g., boys should not play hopscotch and girls cannot play football; men should work and women should stay at home).

Machista: In Spanish culture, the male conservative belief that women are inferior to men in traditionally male-dominated areas such as the workforce, sports, and/or academia. Machistas believe that a woman's place is in the home, while men work; and that men are entitled to cheat on their girlfriends or wives, while women must remain faithful.

Marianismo: The main ideas surrounding marianismo are in direct response to machismo, where a woman possesses the feminine traits of passivity, sexual purity, and selflessness. Based on the Catholic beliefs of Mary, who is both a virgin and a Madonna, marianismo contends that women are spiritually and morally superior to men, and are able to endure extreme sacrifices and suffering for the sake of family. Likewise, women are to remain pure and abstain from sexual activity unless for the purpose of becoming impregnated.

Resiliency: Descriptions of resilience vary across the research. While no exact definition of the term exists, it generally refers to a set of personal traits that enable an individual to successfully adapt and productively transform in the face of adversity.

School-esteem: Feelings of assurance and approval of one's competencies with regard to four school-related dimensions: language (speaking, writing, reading and listening); cognition (learning); motor skills (both fine and large physical movement); and social (interpersonal and intrapersonal relationships). Students with high school-esteem tend to do well academically and socially. Those with low school-esteem can suffer academically and socially, leading to frustration, academic failure, and withdrawal (i.e., dropping out).

Social construction(s): Socially created phenomena (i.e., things, facts, concepts, events) that are agreed to exist (often unconsciously) by a particular society or culture and that has certain behaviors and conventional rules ascribed to them. Examples of social constructs include race, class, gender, age, sexual orientation, and religious affiliation. Key to the perpetuation of social constructions is a group's belief that their social selves are attached to and dependent upon their existence.

Treated: To be insulted, embarrassed, or disrespected by someone.

Womanhood: In some cultural groups, a girl's first menstruation indicates her transition into womanhood. From a sociological standpoint, the concept of womanhood, within traditional Euro-American communities, has changed over the centuries, moving from early ideals of obeying the dictates of males and tending to domestic affairs to contemporary notions of being financially independent, self-reliant, free-thinking, and free-acting. Definitions of womanhood differ across cultures and include a varied set of descriptors like "lady-like," "respectable," and "decent," as well as "savvy," "self-assured," "aggressive," and "competitive."

About the Authors

Horace R. Hall

PhD, is assistant professor at DePaul University in the Department of Educational Policy Studies and Research. He is also the founder and co-director of the school-based youth mentoring program R.E.A.L. (Respect, Excellence, Attitude and Leadership), which is designed to engage young people in critical thinking and social activism.

Dr. Andrea Brown-Thirston

earned her bachelor of science degree from Northwestern University and her doctoral degree in curriculum and instruction from the University of Illinois at Chicago. She is currently chief academic officer for the Chicago International Charter School Network.

Breinigsville, PA USA
09 January 2011
252922BV00001B/1/P